Reach Out
for New Life

BOOKS BY DR. SCHULLER AVAILABLE IN THIS SPECIAL EDITION

Living Positively One Day at a Time
Love or Loneliness . . . You Decide
Reach Out for New Life
Your Future is Your Friend

Reach Out for New Life

Dr. Robert H. Schuller

The Cathedral Press
Garden Grove, California

ISBN: 1-879989-02-6

Published by The Cathedral Press, Crystal Cathedral Ministries,
13280 Chapman Avenue, Garden Grove, California 92640.

Bible passages are from the *Authorized (King James) Version* except those
marked RSV, which are from the *Revised Standard Version*, copyright © 1946,
1952, 1973.

Text design by Wanda Pfloog
Set in ITC Berkeley by Classic Typography

Printed in the United States of America

To My New Readers

I am especially pleased that this book, along with several others, is again available. A number of members and friends of the Crystal Cathedral Ministries have indicated an interest in having them back in print and we are pleased that we were able to comply with their requests.

Since these books were first written and published, there have been many changes in the world and in our lives. Some of the wonderful people from whom I have learned are no longer with us. My children are now all grown and enrich our lives every day.

At first I thought I would revise these books but as our ministry continues to grow, finding the time to do so was almost impossible. Then I realized that revision wasn't really necessary—the references and illustrations are as valid as ever in calling our attention to the everlasting Gospel. I hope you will find this book a life-enriching and live changing experience.

ROBERT SCHULLER

Contents

**Reach Out
for New Life**

1 The Gateway to the Great Way

Welcome Reader! You are about to enter the great way of living that we call Possibility Thinking.

You will meet beautiful, attractive, exciting, stimulating, inspiring people as you begin this journey. You will even meet a new *you*! Your life will – if you really want it to – change directions.

Where are you today? Standing still? Sliding downhill? Spinning your wheels? Are you just moving along slowly? Or are you surging ahead? If you are not moving ahead with power, than this book is for you. I want to show you how you can turn your life around, how you can have turn-around power.

Turnaround Power

A company that makes heavy earth-moving machinery advertises that one of its huge pieces of equipment has "turnaround power." That's what you have – turnaround power. Maybe you haven't discovered it yet, or touched the right button. But I believe that if you read this book you will spot this button, push it, and turn your life around.

You were meant to live an enabling, exciting life, to come finally to a happy ending, with pride behind you, love around you, and hope ahead of you. There's a greatness latent within you destined to come out if you walk the great way we call Possibility Thinking.

Michelangelo attempted forty-four statues in his life, but he finished only fourteen of them. You are familiar with some of them – David in Florence Square, the Pieta, and Moses, to mention a few of the best known. But the thirty he did not finish are interesting, too. You can see them in a museum in Italy . . . a huge chunk of marble from which he sculpted only an elbow or the beginning of a wrist. Another shows a leg, the thigh, the knee, the calf, the foot – even the toes. The rest of the body is locked in. It will never come out. Another reveals a head and shoulders, but the arm and hands are still frozen inside. Could this be true for you? Of all the tragedies in life, the greatest is for a person to live and die and never come out of himself – never to realize the possibilities hidden within.

It was wintertime when Brother Lawrence made a great discovery, which led to his conversion. He stood looking at a tree, naked, barren, and cold. When he touched a twig, it snapped and fell to the snow-covered ground. As he stared at it, he thought, "This tree isn't dead – it just appears to be at this time of the year. In the spring the strength within it will surge forth. New buds will sprout on the dead branches and beautiful new leaves will unfold. The dead looking tree will come back to life . . . "

"There is a destiny," said Brother Lawrence, "there is an energy, there is a force, there is a power and it is good. Its name . . . God." He is here—just ahead of you! He can revive your old dreams. You can come alive again also if you are, today, in the wintertime phase of your life.

How can it happen? How can new life surge within you? Dr. H. E. Gruber, who has conducted a study of draft resisters in the United States during the Vietnam war era, said, "I thought they would fit a personality type, or a political thinking pattern," but added, "not so!" He then told of a young man he felt was typical, someone who was turned around in his own thinking by reading only a few pages in a paperback book while standing at a bookrack in a drugstore. There was no profound learning experience, no extensive counseling, but simply an idea, a thought, a small suggestion, which triggered off a new direction in his life. In that moment he stopped going one way and started going in a totally different direction.

That's what can happen to you. Dr. Gruber might have added that God, our Creator, designed the human being—you—with deep, permanent, sudden conversion capability—turnaround power.

That's what I want for you, and for every person I meet or can influence in some other way. I want more than anything for God to use me in some small or large way to show you the better life God wants you to live. So let's begin with a question: Are you really content to live the rest of your life the way you are living right now?

If your answer is "Yes, I'm content," then you have a problem. You are selling your life too cheaply, and that's a sin. But if your answer is "No, I'm not content to live the rest of my life the way it is today," then you have some great, even fantastic, possibilities ahead of you. You are ready for the turnaround—for God to turn your life around. This life-renewing experience happens as you discover the Power of Possibility Thinking.

The Possibility Thinking Process

In this book I want to share with you a process—the Possibility Thinking Process—which will lead to permanent, creative change in your life. I will show you this process step by step in detail, but here's a hint—a hint of how you will be changed, become the new person God intended you to be.

1. You will begin by believing that there is a more exciting life ahead of you, that there is more in store for your life than what you experience today. You will begin to see that there is more knowledge, more happiness, new opportunities, higher happiness, greater prosperity, richer self-esteem waiting for you. A new *you* will be born with unlimited power.

2. You will become *aware,* and then *beware,* of the negative forces in your life, which have been putting you down and holding you back. You will discover that there is one person in particular who has been the villain. That person, you will discover, is *you.* When you learn that, you are ready to move ahead.

3. You will begin to want to change. Your defensive ego will be softened, your stubborn streaks (we all have some) will begin to yield, and you will be liberated from "locked-in thinking." You will develop new friends for life. They will strengthen, support and rescue you.

4. You will become conscious of your blind spots, your major weaknesses, and you will begin to believe you can correct them. Your biggest problems will be identified, and you will start working on them today—now! And work on them every day of your life. That will be the beginning, the start of incredible miracles happening in your life.

You will suddenly realize that the reason you never changed before was because you didn't want to. For you allowed these negative habits to attach themselves like leeches until you were trapped in a destructive relationship. Now you will be ready to ditch these addictive enemies in your life at any cost. Yes, you now sense a born-again desire to step into the gateway to the great way.

5. Now new dreams, fresh ideas will come into your mind. You will believe that God has a beautiful purpose for your life. And wonder of wonders, you relax, meditate, pray, believe, wait, listen. New possibility thoughts will break into your life—impossible dreams! Impossible? Great! That means it comes from God. You dream only safe dreams, safe ideas, all by yourself. The Big, Beautiful, Risky dreams come from God. He alone gives us "Impossible Ideas—Dreams." It's his way of forcing you out of the "Security Arena" and into the "Faith Arena," where you stop standing still, or sliding back, and start moving ahead with power—come alive power.

6. Now you affirm: "It's Possible!" You may have tried before

and failed, but this time it will be different. You are a different person—older, wiser, more mature, more determined. You
are reading different books, meeting different people, gain-
ing new insights into yourself. You affirm that you were your
own worst enemy, but you have changed already and are going to become your own best friend. And you will succeed.
You will turn an impossibility into a possibility just as a cater-
pillar turns into a butterfly. How?

7. You develop a plan to cooperate with your new dreams.
You give God your enthusiastic and full support in making
the miracle happen. What will it take to turn Impossibility
into Possibility in terms of money, determination, brain power,
contracts, education, time, self-discipline, self-denial, and self-
sacrifice? In this phase of the Possibility Thinking process you
make your final determination on the price you are willing
to pay to succeed. Do that and you are ready to move on
to the next step.

8. You establish a calendar. Put down a starting date and
announce it to people who would be shocked if you didn't
keep your word. Then put down a review date, giving yourself enough time to measure your progress.

9. You build in personal rewards and punishments. Promise
yourself a treat as you pay the price. Inflict on yourself a dis-
agreeable treatment if you cheat yourself. The self-inflicted
punishment must be far more distasteful than the price you
are prepared to pay to succeed.

Allow Your Head to Lead Your Heart

You can see that as you use the Possibility Thinking process
your head will lead your heart. You will never succeed if you

begin with your *feelings*. You will use your head to program your heart. Concentrate on what you need to do to succeed. Program yourself to lose your desire for whatever blocks you from succeeding.

When I had a weight problem I loved doughnuts and sweet rolls. Today I can't stand them. They are too sweet and sticky. Now I *want* naturally sweet fruits.

In college I smoked two packs of cigarettes a day until I learned how that habit was threatening me with lung cancer. So I programmed myself to discover the ugly taste in tobacco. After three years my heart took over, and I no longer *wanted* to smoke. Now I prefer the sweet, clean, delicious taste of fresh air around my tongue, teeth, and deep within my lungs.

Not only was I overweight and smoked too much, but I was also physically out of shape. So I used my head and told myself to *do* what was best for me, and eventually I became addicted to what was best for me. I began to run several miles a day, and today I thoroughly enjoy it. In Paris, when I visited there, I ran several miles around the Eiffel Tower. In Switzerland I rose at dawn and ran around the lake. Wherever I am there is a place to run, and I enjoy it. But more important, I no longer enjoy the alternative—just sitting, slouched in a chair. That really makes me feel old.

In your own turnaround, just ahead of you, you will literally alter and change your feelings! Your tastes! Your desires! That's the exciting turnaround power that waits for you as you enter the Gateway to the Great Way.

It's time to get started. Now! Let's start with a personality test to find out who you are and where you are, so you will know yourself. Before a student is admitted to college he takes an entrance exam. It's only a checkup to establish one's own starting point. So be honest. Remember–if you cheat, you cheat only yourself, and you are the last person you want to be the victim of cheating. So begin–now!

Personality Profile Questionnaire

1. What kind of person are you?
   _____I believe in improvement.
   _____I am satisfied with things as they are.
   _____I believe "It can be done better."
   _____I think, "It's good enough."
   _____I don't think I have any serious problems.
   _____I think I could be a more beautiful person if I could change in some areas.
   _____I want to become aware of my shortcomings, and believe I'm not too old, too lazy or set-in-my ways to change.
   _____I don't want to change.
2. What kind of a person would you like to be?
   (Take the time–right now–to write your answer or draw a picture.)
3. What plans would you make today if you were sure you could succeed?
   (Another essay question. Answer carefully.)
4. Do you believe you have the freedom to be either a possibility thinker or an impossibility thinker?
   Yes_____ No_____
5. Have you ever entertained a great possibility?
   Yes_____ No_____

6. Did you:
   _____Try it and succeed?
   _____Reject it—knew it was impossible?
   _____Talk to a few people who put it down before you tried it yourself?
   _____Try, but run into problems and quit?
7. If you quit, did you give up because you didn't have enough:
   _____Money?
   _____Training?
   _____Contacts?
   _____Organization?
   _____Time?
   _____Energy?
   _____Health?
8. Or did you lose your enthusiasm and belief in the dream?
   Yes_____ No_____
9. If you gave up, do you now believe that if you had enough time, wisdom, money, emotional strength, outside support from your colleagues, family, and friends that you might possibly have succeeded—if you kept on keeping on?
   Yes_____ No_____
10. What dreams would you commit yourself to today if you knew that you could tap an unlimited source of creative intelligence, if you had access to unlimited personal financing, if you could be introduced to powerful friends who would listen and help you?
    (Another essay question. Take your time.)
11. Are you willing to read the rest of this book and honestly try to apply its principles?
    Yes_____ No_____

If you answered the last question with a *yes*, you passed! You are about to break loose! You have stepped through the Gateway and into the Great Way! The Possibility Thinking Process is working within you already.

2 Become a Supersuccessful Person

Turnaround people follow a rule they never break – they focus on *possibilities* rather than on *problems*. Like a plant that bends toward the light in order to grow, they run from the darkness to the light. You have, I believe, turned that corner in your life. You are running toward the sunrise of a new way of thinking, with new concepts and new ideas.

Supersuccessful People aren't usually "born with silver spoons in their mouths." They are, in fact, frequently born in poverty, ignorance, and darkness. But they have one thing in common. They run toward the sunrise, toward the light of opportunity, wherever it shines.

You too can become a Supersuccessful Person. What do I mean by success?

Success does not mean, necessarily, reaching all of your goals. It is rather a matter of developing your hidden potential.

Success doesn't mean solving all your problems. On the contrary, as a Supersuccessful Person you will produce bigger challenges. You do eliminate old problems; you exchange them for more exciting problems that are actually possibilities in disguise.

Success isn't the opposite of failing. A runner may come in last, but if he beats his best record, he still succeeds.

Success isn't measured by the money you accumulate. To be sure, since honest success is the result of meeting authentic human need, it often follows that Supersuccessful People become wealthy people. In a world that cries for money to eliminate poverty, ignorance, and disease, we may hope there will be many persons who acquire wealth in order to build a healthier and happier human community. But no matter how wealthy Supersuccessful People become, they never forget that "being" is more important than "getting." What you *are* is more important than what you *have*. I have a friend who has set a goal of making a million dollars in order to give it all away. Now that's a Supersuccessful idea.

My Definition of Success

I have a simple definition of success: *"Success is building self-esteem in yourself and others through sincere service."* We could say: Success is self-respect. It's that wonderful feeling that comes to you when you have helped others help themselves to a better and more beautiful life.

Now we see why success is so important. Because the alternative is failure, and failure is disastrous to a person's self-esteem. Without a successful experience you will remain forever trapped in the impoverished ghetto of a negative self-image. Success turns you around from being a nonself-loving person into a positive person with healthy self-love.

All Supersuccessful People know that self-esteem is life's highest value. They know the joy of *getting* is being able to *give* to those in need. They know the joy of sharing the fruits of success. This great joy is the experience of self-esteem. So building self-esteem in yourself is both the motive and the measure of success.

That's why I challenge you to get set and join the Super-success circle. Whoever you are, wherever you are, I invite you to climb the success ladder, all the way to the top.

Regardless of the circumstances!

"Under the circumstances she did quite well," a supervisor said, pointing to a worker who came from an impoverished background. "She's a great Possibility Thinker," he added proudly. "That's the reason she is a success."

"But as a Possibility Thinker she wasn't *under* the circumstances—she climbed *above* them—even *on* them," I replied.

In every facet of your life there is a ladder—your community, your company, your profession, trade, or career. On every one of those ladders there is someone at the top, someone at the bottom, and still others in between. You are on that ladder somewhere. On the top, on the bottom, or somewhere in between.

If you follow the Possibility Thinking process outlined in this book, I guarantee that you will climb higher on your ladder than you ever climbed before. You will rise higher than you ever believed was possible for you. What a great feeling of proper pride, of humble self-respect you will have!

Why is it that some people are at the top, some are at the bottom, and others in between? Is it because of *talents?*

Not really. I can prove to you that talent is not the major ingredient in success. All you need to do is look around and see others in your own profession—doctors, truck drivers, salespersons, teachers, politicians. Some you will find are higher on the ladder than you, and you know that you have more talent than they do. And you can see people at the bottom of the ladder who have more talent than you do. Look! Around the bottom of every ladder of every career and profession are many talented people who aren't going anywhere.

On a plane one day I discovered that my seatmate was from Green Bay, Wisconsin. "Oh, I've heard of that," I said. "But what does Green Bay have besides the Packers?" "I don't know," he said, "As far as I am concerned, Green Bay *is* the Packers. You see, I'm the coach." Trying to keep the conversation going, I asked, "How's the team going to do next season?" "Great," he said, "we've got talent." (Ah, I thought, now I'm going to learn the secret I've been looking for.) "What's talent?" I asked. "That's a good question," he replied. "I don't really know, but I would guess it's character. Young men who are basically clean, wholesome, and good. And because of this they have drive, yes, that's it! The drive to win is the talent." Are top of the ladder people more talented? No, unless you want to describe talent as drive and character. Only people with character have the drive to reach for the top. And the exciting thing is, character is something anybody can develop.

Other underachievers complain that success is dependent on *territory,* where one happens to live. But that's not necessarily true, either. Supersuccessful people are not great achievers because of *where* they are but because of *what* they are. As persons with admirable character, they have learned how to use power for the good of other people. And that is what character is, really. A study of success is, when you get right down to it, a study in the flow of power, who acquires power, how power is used, won, held, restrained, managed. A Supersuccessful Person is a person with power. And power never flows to places. Power always flows to people.

Not long ago I visited Persepolis, one of the more forgotten and forsaken places on planet Earth. It's in Persia—Iran as we know it today—midway between the Persian Gulf and Teheran. You would expect Teheran to be a great city because of its geography. But Persepolis, far off the beaten path, was the power center of the world during the reigns of Cyrus I and Cyrus II. What made this city great? Not the place, but the people there. So mark this carefully. *Power never gravitates to places; power always gravitates to people.*

The owner of a hardware store in Watertown, New York, once had a problem with which many merchants are familiar. He had a lot of items in his store he couldn't sell. A young boy who worked for the merchant had an idea. "Why don't we put it all on a table out on the sidewalk and stick up a sign that says, 'ten cents or less—take your choice!'" The owner tried to put down the idea, saying, "People will think because the merchandise is so cheap it's falling apart; they won't buy it, not even for ten cents." The kid said, "The idea might work, it just might work." (These are the three most important words you will ever learn: *It might work!* They start the Possibility Thinking Process to work.) The negative thinking merchant finally agreed to try the idea.

So the boy put the items on the sidewalk, along with his ten cent sign. In no time everything was sold. The boy said, "Let's do it again," but the boss said, "No, it won't work the second time." Well, the kid got disgusted, quit his job, and started his own business, calling it a "five and ten cent store." Years later, he became one of the most successful merchandisers in American history. His name, F. W. Woolworth. His figure can be found sculpted in bronze, outside of the Merchandise Mart in Chicago, as one of the nine greatest merchants in United States history.

Supersuccess. It's not *talent* and it's not *territory*. It isn't a matter of *tricks* either. You think you have to be able to manipulate people in order to be a good salesperson? Not so! Successful selling is nothing more than communicating to people a truth they weren't aware of before. A salesperson is a servant of others. You don't have to con people or bribe them with gimmicks. You only need an honest product people really need. Honesty releases enthusiasm. Enthusiasm is drive. So great determination is generated. The Supersuccessful Person dreams, makes decisions, lays plans, sets goals, and determines that he will not fail. That's what Possibility Thinking is all about.

My favorite success story is about a little girl named Tara. While her parents were taking a few days' vacation, they received an urgent message to call Children's Hospital in Orange County, California, immediately. Tara, they learned, had fallen and had been brought to the hospital in critical condition. As soon as they reached the medical center, they heard over the public address system the call, "99, 99," which means that every doctor on duty has to rush to the room. Somebody is dying. It was Tara. They pulled her through that time, but they were to hear the call "99, 99, 99" again for Tara. Six times her heart stopped. But each time she was brought back to life.

Alive! But not much more than a vegetable. That's the way they took her home. One night her parents, Mike and Donna, were at her bedside when Mike put his fingers around her lips and recited a favorite rhyme, "Bumblebee, bumblebee, fly around the tree," And, miracle of miracles, she smiled! Her first sign of response.

But that was the only response for awhile. Although Tara's parents believed she could, somehow, recover, she showed no further improvement. They bathed her, dressed her, tried to put food in her mouth—and loved her. Then they learned of the Institute of Human Potential in Philadelphia, where Dr. Glen Doman checked her over carefully. "Yes, we might be able to do something for her, but you have to pattern her eight hours every day," he said. "It will take four people moving her head, pulling her arms, pulling her legs. Maybe we can teach her undamaged brain cells to take over and function," he said. "She just might learn to talk again," he added, cautiously.

I remember the first time I saw Tara. By this time she had regained her sight and speech. When I came to see her she was in her therapy room, ready for her patterning exercise.

"Are you ready, Tara?" her mother asked. And Tara began to sing with perfect diction, "Jesus loves me, this I know. For the Bible tells me so. We are weak, but he is strong. . . . " Her singing set the rhythm for the women who were forcing her body to exercise in the reenactment of a child's crawl. I walked out of the room thinking of people who once had a dream and gave up because it was too hard, or they thought they couldn't do it, or it wouldn't work.

Success – A Quality of the Mind

What, precisely, are the mental qualifications that make up Possibility Thinking for Supersuccess? Are we talking about Intelligence Quotient? Not so! In Rudyard Kipling's words, "First prizes don't always go to the brightest and strongest; again and again the person who wins is the one who is sure he can." Following are qualities of mind that cause people to become Possibility Thinkers.

Supersuccessful Possibility Thinkers are *progressive* people. Such a person can be characterized by these principles:

- **A PROGRESSIVE PERSON BELIEVES HE NEEDS TO IMPROVE**

Are you willing to admit that you do make mistakes? That there are times when you have been wrong in your judgment? Are you willing to admit that you have blind spots? That you have been indoctrinated, brainwashed, and prejudiced in some of your attitudes and viewpoints? If so, you have the first mark of a progressive person. Join me in saying, right now, "I am not perfect. I make mistakes. I commit errors of judgment. I have a blind spot and may not even be aware of my major mistakes."

- **A PROGRESSIVE PERSON SEEKS CONSTRUCTIVE CRITICISM AND CORRECTION**

To improve, we have to discover our weak spots. I try to find my own. In my own ministry at the Garden Grove Community Church and over the Hour of Power television program, I make a practice of reading a digest of all my negative mail. You see, I think the "complaint" department is really our "quality control" department. That's important for Possibility Thinking. We must learn to admit that we are imperfect. It conditions us to welcome insight into our "problem areas." For we need to know where our weaknesses are if we are to improve and spare ourselves from the negative results of personal mistakes. Are you willing to take the same attitude? A progressive person is anxious to get constructive criticism from his friends because he knows they really want to help him.

- ### THE PROGRESSIVE PERSON ADMITS PUBLICLY HIS SHORTCOMINGS, FAILING, AND MISTAKES

This means saying out loud a sentence that more than anything else marks you as an adult: "You are right, and I was wrong." When you are ready to do that, you are on the edge of a miracle that will change you as a person at the very deepest level. And marvel of marvels, you will hear the words: "I forgive you. . . . You are forgiven!"

Suddenly you begin to change. You become a new person, an open person, a free person. No longer do you try to give people the impression that you are perfect. The defensive stance of an insecure person is dropped. The arrogance is gone. Suddenly you stand there as an honest, humble human being, who is heard to say, "Maybe I am the head of the history department, but I don't know it all, and I hope to keep learning and growing." When that happens, a remarkable change begins to take place in your life. Your phoney masks are gone. You stop playing games. You give up your false pretending. That's the start of the miracle. A bridge is built where there was a chasm. A wall is torn down. Tensions are dissolved. Communication is restored. A fracture is mended. Polarization turns into dialogue. Suspicion gives way to trust. New life begins.

Supersuccessful people, because they are progressive people, break free from "locked-in thinking."

It's a fact. Failure-prone low achievers are infected with impossibility thinking, which we call boxed-in, locked-in, thinking: "A rigid mind-set," that could be described as "frozen attitudes," or "concretized thinking."

There are four mental fences that keep your creativity locked in, trapped.

These nonmoral, nonethical, nonlegal, nonreligious boundaries form "fences" that trap creativity and progress up the ladder of Success.

Let's examine them more closely.

- PERSONAL LIMITATIONS

Do you lack education? Money? Experience? So what? Join the club. Everyone has personal limitations. Everyone is a beginner sometime, somewhere. Rembrandt was once a beginner. So was Einstein. You have suffered failure or rejection? Don't worry about it. Every successful writer, experimenter, and inventor has failed too. It's not the failures that count, but what you learn from them that matters. There is an answer to each of your personal problems. There is someone, somewhere, who can help you overcome your limitations.

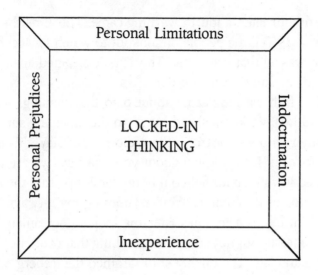

Personal Limitations

Personal Prejudices

LOCKED-IN
THINKING

Indoctrination

Inexperience

• **INDOCTRINATION**

A classic example of indoctrination is the sinking of the Titanic, a tragedy that sent 1,516 people to a watery grave in
1912. Locked-in thinking is what destroyed their lives. They
were locked-in because they followed the crowd. They lacked
the capacity for independent thinking.

Three days after this beautiful "unsinkable" ship was out
of Queenstown, a wire was received that told of icebergs in
the ship's path. But the wireless operator ignored the message. He had been told the ship was unsinkable, so why should
he bother? That's locked-in thinking right there. Hours later
another cable came with the same message. The wireless operator heard it, but failed to write it down. A third message
came. This time the operator wrote it down, handed it to the
captain, who read it and, without comment, turned it over
to the managing director of the White Star Line, who looked
at it and threw it in the wastebasket on the bridge.

An hour later, a fourth warning came. This time the captain said, "Tell the people on lookout to watch for icebergs." That was all that was done. The Titanic steamed ahead, full speed, 22 knots, into the darkness.

The fifth warning came about 9:30 that evening. Still no slowdown, 22 knots ahead. At 11:30 the crackling sound of another ship was heard in the radio room: "Hey, this is the Californian. I don't know about you, but boy, we are really locked in with an ice field out here." "Shut up," said the radio operator of the Titanic, "You're jamming my airways," and cut him off. Ten minutes later the lookout screamed, "Iceberg ahead!" But now there was nothing that could be done. It was too late. The mighty ship rammed the iceberg, which cut a gash 300 feet long. All sixteen watertight compartments were immediately sealed off, and everybody said, "We will be all right. It's unsinkable." But one bulkhead gave way, then another, and the ship was doomed.

Meanwhile, passengers were told the ship was in danger, that they should head for the lifeboats. But, never in the whole cruise had the passengers been assigned to a lifeboat. After all, what was the need for that? The Titanic was unsinkable! (That's what you call locked-in thinking.) When the announcement came that the ship was in danger of sinking, and for the people to go to lifeboats, many of them refused to obey the orders. Why should they? The Titanic was unsinkable! Testimony later showed that the lifeboats could have accommodated at least 500 more passengers – people who were sure the Titanic would stay afloat. Locked-in thinking! Indoctrination! Indoctrinated people don't think. They merely react. For them, creative problem-solving is impossible. The course is set for failure and disaster.

• INEXPERIENCE

"There is no substitute for experience." True, but never let inexperience become an excuse for nonachievement. Possibility Thinkers are adventurers, and all of them begin at precisely the same place – inexperience. Every Superstar in the Big Leagues, whether in sports, industry, education, the arts, science, or religion, started as a rookie. Think of the colossal waste of human potential, energy, growth, and creativity that occurs when we allow inexperience to hold us back. To become a Supersuccessful Person you need to be an adventurer. Like Karen.

Karen left her parents home a few days after high school graduation to "try her wings." But she had no well-defined plan, and a few days later she was broke. Getting more desperate by the minute, she bought an apple for her lunch and sat down on a curb in Princeton, New Jersey, seriously wondering if she hadn't made a big mistake in leaving the home where her parents would care for her. Then she noticed a man painting the curb nearby, and she went over to ask him, "Are there more jobs like that? I can paint."

"Not that I know of," the man said, "but if you want a job, the taxi folks over on the corner are looking for a driver." So Karen went there and applied. "Have you a driver's license?" the man asked. She had, had never been in an accident, and had a good driving record to boot.

"Okay," the man said, "fill out these forms and we will hire you." In a few days the paper work was done, and Karen reported to work. "What do I do first?" she asked. "Well," the manager drawled, "you can take a load of foreign dignitaries who have been visiting Princeton University to Kennedy Airport in New York, use the limo."

Later, Karen told of the experience–or, better, inexperience. "I was literally shaking," she said. "I didn't know if I could handle a limousine. I didn't even know my way to Kennedy Airport. And my passengers didn't either. All I could do was to look at a map hurriedly and start out, hoping I wouldn't mess up. Believe me, I became a pro in a hurry."

Inexperience can only hurt you if you don't do something about it. And the beautiful thing is, you can. You have the freedom to choose to try.

• PREJUDICE

Prejudice locks in your thinking, if nothing else does. On your way to becoming a Possibility Thinker, you are becoming aware of the areas of your life where you mentally exercise the blight of prejudice. It's a character defect not alone because of the way your prejudice devalues other people, other cultures, other social orders. Just as important, if not more important, is the way your prejudice keeps you from progressing up the ladder to becoming a Supersuccessful Person.

Because of prejudice the voice of Marian Anderson was long denied on the great concert stages of our country.

Because of prejudice great athletes of the past were denied opportunity to perform in the stadiums and arenas of our land.

Because of prejudice young people with great minds have been denied opportunity to excel in our schools.

But there's more. Because of prejudice we deny ourselves the chance to know and befriend people of greatness–people of minority races and others our society puts down but who wouldn't put themselves down. We deny ourselves the opportunity to grow from the richness they have to offer us.

So release your mind from indoctrinated prejudices that keep you from discovering some of life's richest possibilities.

Supersuccess – Make It Happen Now

Locked-in thinkers are people who sit around waiting for success to happen, and when it doesn't they complain.

I am thinking of two salesmen. One works for an auto agency. Every time I drop by I see him sitting behind a desk with his legs crossed. "How's business?" I ask. He answers, glumly, "Oh, pretty good."

The other salesman is of a different sort. When I ask him how business is, he says, "Great!" But he doesn't sit behind a desk. When I come around, I find him on the telephone, working on a prospect list. He's adding names of people that could possibly need what he's selling. Good salesmen make sales happen. People who live a superlife make it super. They plant seeds, make calls, write letters. They are aggressive, on the move. They don't wait for success to find them. They find success.

The great Danish philosopher, Sören Kierkegaard, once told a story of a flock of geese that was starting to head South to escape the blast of wintry winds. The first night they landed in a farmer's yard and filled themselves with corn. Next morning they flew on–all, that is, except one. "The corn is good," this big goose said, "so I will stay and enjoy it another day." The next morning he decided to wait still another day, and another after that, enjoying the delicious food. Pretty soon he had developed a habit. "Tomorrow I will fly South," he said.

Then came the inevitable day when the winds of winter were so severe that waiting longer would mean death in the frozen wastes. So he stretched his wings and waddled across the barnyard, picking up speed as he went. But alas! He was too fat to fly. He had waited too long. *Decide today to acquire the mental qualifications of the Supersuccessful Person.*

Determine to be progressive. Determine to break loose from your locked-in thinking.

Now comes the third mental qualification of a Possibility Thinker–an inspired Self-confidence.

3 Take a
Pause for Applause

What you need now – more than anything else – is overpowering confidence. Supersuccess depends on it. To have it, you need a deep belief in your latent, God-given, possibilities.

The image you have of yourself, more than anything else, will determine how you learn, what you read, and what entertainment you seek. Your self-image will determine the wife or husband you select, your career, your job, and your attitude toward it. Your self-concept is the core of your personality. God wants you to have a positive self-concept. In short, confidence.

It's incredible how some people put themselves down. They even use religion to help them. Some people think that's humility. Maybe it is, in a perverse kind of way, but the person who goes around praying, "Oh, God, I am nothing," is not a Christian. That kind of humility is a distortion of Christianity.

St. Paul writes:

"For I know whom I have believed, and am persuaded that he is able to keep that which I have committed unto him against that day" (2 Tim. 1:12).

"I can do all things through Christ who strengthens me" (Phil. 4:13).

"I urge you, then, be imitators of me" (1 Cor. 4:16).

Humility? Very much so, because he knows his strength is rooted in God. But he's confident!

Confidence! That's what you need. It is the bottom line quality of the Possibility Thinker.

A teacher in a public school said to her students, "Today we are going to study identity." To Johnny, a black youngster who grew up in a ghetto community, she asked, "You know what that means? It's who you really are. Can you tell me who *you* are?" He stood up and said, "My name is Johnny Jones. And I know I'm black. And I know I'm beautiful, because God don't make no junk."

You, too, can have that kind of confidence. It comes with deep belief in God. Convinced that God created you with tremendous undiscovered and undeveloped possibilities, you will suddenly rise to a self-confidence that will give you power to transcend obstacles, prejudices, handicaps, and setbacks.

Shy, timid, inferiority plagued people are like the California desert in December. In the winter it is a dry, barren, and bleak place. But hidden in the beige wasteland are millions of seeds, just waiting for the spring rains to make them come alive, and turn the desert into miles of blooming flower beds.

In your mind and mine are talent possibilities that wait,

like dry seed on a winter desert, for the spring rains to come. Once you know who you are, that you are part of God's family, you will have an immense new birth of selfworth. So pin a label on yourself: "God's child—Treat with Respect!" Stop putting yourself down. Take a pause for applause. You're somebody!

Would you believe you are a potential genius? In Chapter 1, I mentioned a meeting of the International Psychological Congress in Paris. The delegates heard a report on a study of child prodigies, which said, "Our research shows that child prodigies are *developed*. That is, they were and are nurtured, trained until unbelievable and most extraordinary accomplishments begin to emerge." Think of that! It means that average human beings have the possibility of becoming near-geniuses. You have that potentiality!

Ralph Bunche, the first black to win the Nobel Peace Prize, overcame innumerable obstacles in his rise to prominence as a leading American statesman. His mother died when he was very young, and his father died soon after. He was left an orphan at the age of twelve.

When his parents died, he left his home in Detroit and came to Los Angeles to live with his grandmother, Lucy Johnson. She was an inspiration, and near the end of her life her writings were put in a small book, entitled *Believe in Yourself*. "Never say I am going to try, but, rather, I am going to do," she wrote. "To achieve you must possess self-confidence." There is the secret of Ralph Bunche's success. It was his grandmother who planted the seed of self-belief deep into this twelve-year-old black orphan boy. It made all the difference. Self-confidence rooted in religious beliefs moves mountains.

In Calcutta, a young man introduced himself to me as Dwight Dobson. "Are you a missionary?" I asked. "Sort of," he replied. I invited him to tell his story.

"I felt called by God to come to India," he began. "So I asked for an application to come, only India wouldn't allow missionaries to enter the country. But I felt so strongly that God was guiding me here that my wife and I decided to come anyway. So we got a 120-day tourist visa. After we had been in the country all but five of those days, we knew the door was closed. So we made reservations to fly back to the United States.

"The day before we were to leave, my wife came down with dysentery. Too sick to travel, we made arrangements for a later flight. An hour after our original flight left, the telephone rang. The voice at the other end of the line said, 'Hello, I am the police commissioner of Calcutta.' My heart sank. I wondered what I was going to do. The voice said, 'I want you to come to my office right away.'

"I went there, half scared to death. The police commissioner said, 'I understand you are a karate and judo expert, is that right?' I said, 'Yes, sir, I am.' 'Isn't it rather odd for an ordained minister to be a black belt expert?' he asked. So I told him that when I was in high school there was a teacher who told us to learn judo, that it would come in handy some day. So we did, and our team went to the Nationals, where we all won the black belt.

"The commissioner, unaware of my fear, then said: 'I have a problem. Over two thousand of my street police officers have been killed in the past three years by Communists in this city. Would you stay here and train my officers in judo to help them protect themselves?' 'I can't get a visa,' I said.

The police commissioner said, 'I think I can arrange that.' That was two years ago and since that time I have trained 5,500 policement in judo. In the past year the deaths have been cut to nil, and the Communists have failed to create total chaos by breaking up the police department."

What saved the city? One young man who taught the police unarmed self-defense techniques. But there's more. My new friend continued his narrative. "Because the judo program was so successful, the commissioner finally came to me and said, 'Since you are a minister, if you want to give the police a little Bible lesson, go ahead.'"

Twelve years earlier, when a high school teacher had said, "Why don't you learn judo, it will come in handy," God was guiding.

Nothing generates self-confidence as powerfully as the conviction that you are being guided by God. And it's true! God plans and guides our lives long before we are aware of what is happening.

Self-Confidence Moves Mountains

Over a century ago, John Roebling had a fabulous idea. He believed that it was possible to connect Manhattan Island with Brooklyn by building a huge suspension bridge over the East River. At that time suspension bridges were just becoming known, due to Roebling's invention of wire rope in 1841. But at that time, few people believed that a span of 1,595 feet could be built to withstand the winds and the pressures of the tides. Nothing like it had ever been built before.

Roebling persisted, however, and in 1869 he was appointed chief engineer of the longest bridge-building project in the world. Soon after the work began in 1869, a ferry hit the pilings on which he was standing, and his foot was crushed in the accident. In spite of the amputation of several toes, he died of tetanus a short time after.

But that did not end the dream. Roebling had a son named Washington, who had gone to Europe two years before the accident to learn about the newly invented method of constructing underwater foundations by using caissons filled with compressed air – a method his father hoped to use for the Brooklyn Bridge. After his father's death, young Washington took over as chief engineer. For the next several years he supervised every detail and procedure. He spent long hours in the high pressure of the caissons, and in the spring of 1872 was taken out almost unconscious, after some twelve hours in a compressed air chamber.

His health was permanently damaged, and never again would he come near the bridge site. From then on he stayed at his home in Brooklyn, watching the construction with a telescope from his window. Because he could no longer talk, as a result of the bends he suffered in the compressed air chamber, he developed a code by which he could communicate. He would tap a single finger on the arm of his wife, and in this way he told her what had to be done next. She, in turn, instructed the engineers. For eleven years he supervised its construction in this way. Incredible! But that's how the Brooklyn Bridge was finally built.

When the traffic finally streamed across the span, Washington Roebling watched the ceremony through his telescope from his bedroom window. He couldn't talk and he couldn't laugh, but he could cry. And cry he did.

Some people call that "heart"; others call it determination. I call it self-confidence.

By every standard you can think of, Ethel Waters should have been an emotionally deprived and mentally scarred person. She was conceived in a rape that resulted in her mother's pregnancy. Born an illegitimate child, raised in a ghetto and in poverty, her life puts a lie to the notion that Supersuccesses are born to good fortune. She is one of the most beautiful souls on the whole planet earth. But when you learn of how she was knocked around the alleys of her ghetto and banged around through life, you wonder about her secret. How is it that she has this big, loving bubbling heart?

I will long remember the night I was invited to join the luminaries of Hollywood to salute Ethel Waters. It was a stellar event, but the greatest moment was when Ethel herself, in her inimitable, open, and honest way told people how happy she was "because Jesus is in my heart." I watched her perform that night, listened to her sing, and heard her preach as only she can, and I thought to myself: If there is a contest to determine who is the healthiest person in the world emotionally, Ethel Waters would win hands down. She knows how to laugh and how to cry. She is a big heart, a great soul. . . . she is alive!

Because she was hurt so much as a child, it is no wonder that she always sang, "Stormy Weather," with such feeling. Somebody asked her to sing it that night. But she said, "No,

sir, I'm never going to sing "Stormy Weather" again as long
as I live. I can't! I don't have stormy weather any more. I have
got peace in my heart because Jesus lives in me now."

That's confidence! Superconfidence! Ethel Waters knows
the secret. We were designed by God as beings wherein God
himself could live. You will experience peak emotional health
and wholeness when God lives within you. There is no emotional problem that a God-inspired Positive Self-Image cannot heal. When God touches your life, he lets you know that
you are his idea. When you know that, you are on the road
that leads and lifts you upward and onward. In Ethel Waters'
own words, "God don't sponsor flops!"

Failure Is of Your Own Making

Now let me tell you why you fail. You fail because you deliberately, knowingly, and willingly choose to fail! You choose to
fail because you do not believe you can succeed. Your lack
of trust in yourself provokes an insecurity in your relationships, an insecurity which results first in defensive, then
hostile, behavior, and finally in aggressive conflict of depress-
ing emotional withdrawal and defeat.

The Cause and Cure of a Negative Self-Image

What is the real reason people lack self-confidence? When
theologians say that the core of sin is rebellion against God,
they stop short of the mark. The deeper question is *why* peo-

ple could rebel against a beautiful God. The answer is that every person is born with a negative self-image, which is reflected in an inherent distrust, a fear of failure in relationships. So we tend to rebel, which is to say we set up a defensive mechanism to protect ourselves from a possible relationship we regard as threatening.

Erik Erikson has demonstrated how this process works. The newly born infant is born lacking in trust, he says. In the first stage of his development, until he is a year old, he begins to learn the experience of trust. He passes through the traumatic experience of birth—which is, when you think about it, a rude and shocking way to enter the world—from nontrust to trust. Through soft stroking, bathing, feeding, holding, the new occupant learns that this noisy alien world isn't so horrible after all.

In stage two, until he is two years old, the initial trust becomes self-confidence. The infant learns to crawl and after a time finds that he can stand. Now he feels the thrill of the vertical dimension. He feels tall.

In succeeding stages of his growth, the child is challenged to experience individuality, to discover that he has the ability to make choices, that he has the power to make decisions. And he also learns the rewards of achievement. As achievement piles on achievement, he discovers his selfhood. He tries, fails, tries again, and finally learns. So he moves emotionally from lack of trust, to trust, to self-confidence.

But then, something tragic may happen. This infantile self-belief may be stunted and fail to blossom into its fullest flower. The deep-seated core of distrust may again threaten to assert itself, warning the growing person: "Be careful. You may get hurt." Almost without knowing it, self-confidence begins to disappear in adolescence and adulthood. The resulting caution tends to further throttle and strangulate self-confidence.

Self-confidence becomes supplanted by a fear of failure— which becomes a pattern, a habit. And with what devious results! The fear of failure, rising from a lack of self-trust, becomes a desire to fail. "If I don't try, I'll not fail." "If I just sit there on the end of the bench where the coach won't see me, I won't go up to the plate and strike out." "If I don't try to quit smoking, I won't fail in my efforts to kick the habit." You see how it works. The way to succeed is to fail even to try.

So a negative self-image becomes the major emotional disorder that entangles human beings in a web of failure-producing attitudes. We choose to fail because we don't dare succeed. So we fail because we choose to fail. That's what I mean when I say failure is the product of a deliberate effort.

The Cure for Failure

Who has the cure for this deep inner distrust that returns again and again to haunt us throughout the several stages of our lives? I will tell you the secret. If you will, with sincerity, ask God to guide your life, he will unfold amazing possibilities within your "born-again imagination." New and exciting ideas will come to you. Believe in those ideas, and start believing in yourself.

A stuntman once rigged a tightrope across Niagara Falls and announced that he was going to walk across both ways. A crowd gathered and applauded when he proved his boast.

People who said it couldn't be done now became believers. Then he took a wheelbarrow and did the same thing. Again, the crowd applauded, "Now," he said, "I'm going to ask for a volunteer. Who will ride in the wheelbarrow?" The applauding believers now suddenly drew back. There was silence. But a young girl came forward and said, "I will ride in your wheelbarrow." And she did.

"Of course the girl trusts him," someone observed, "He is her father."

Now that's trust—the kind you must be open to if you are to be a Supersuccess. You will remain an insecure person as long as you try to run your life without the guidance, direction, wisdom, power, and presence of a Higher Power. How can you acquire such trust? Begin now by affirming aloud: "I am becoming a different person. I am God's special idea. And the world has yet to see the great things I can do and the beautiful person I can become."

An enormously powerful self-confidence is rising within you as you turn your life over to God and trust him. He is giving you now a more positive self-image, so that positive ideas will flow naturally through your mind. The greatest force in the world is a positive idea in the self-confident mind of a bold believer who is walking with God and trusting in him.

Trust God. Believe in yourself. Dare to dream. Put your whole future in his hands.

You have heard it said, "I've got to see it before I believe it."

The truth is the other way around: "I've got to believe it before I see it!" Do that and you are on the way to Supersuccess.

Be sure of this: If you will, with profound sincerity, prayerfully ask God to guide your life, he will unfold amazing possibilities within your "born-again imagination." New and exciting ideas will come to you. Now believe in those ideas and believe in yourself.

Don't confuse the person you are with the person you were or the person you will become!

You were an insecure person trying to run your life without God's guidance, direction, wisdom, power, and presence. In that state, you were naturally prone to anxiety and understandably lacking in self-confidence. If recurring self-doubts return to draw you back or hold you back—do not be confused. You are only remembering the person you were.

If you have read this book so far, then you are already a different person. And the world has yet to see what great things you can do and what a beautiful person you can become.

4 The Power of
a Possibility Perspective

The three key mental qualifications of Possibility Thinking we have discussed are: having a progressive attitude; becoming liberated from locked-in thinking; possessing the self-confidence to dare to adventure.

Now we are ready for a fourth element: the absolutely indispensable matter of *perspective*.

An Impossibility Thinker sees everything from a negative perspective: he turns opportunities into obstacles; he looks at projects and imagines difficulties.

I confess that I frequently conspire to turn dedicated Impossibility Thinkers around. One day, while I was waiting for a limousine at the Philadelphia International Airport, I stood next to a gentleman who apparently wanted to get the same transportation. I said to him, "Beautiful weather, beautiful day." "Yeah," he said, "But you should have been here last week." I tried again. "My, the sky is really blue," I said. "Yeah," he replied, "But wait until we get downtown." We stood there in silence for a while, and then I said, really reaching now, "Look at all those cars lined up here. Isn't America a great place, where almost everybody can have his own car?" And guess what he said to me: "Yeah, but they don't make them like they used to." Now there is a truly dedicated Impossibility Thinker.

You see the problem. The gentleman was probably right on all counts—*from his perspective!* His error was in assuming that his perspective was the only perspective; in not being able to see what was happening around him through another set of eyes. Once I saw a television program in which a panel of experts discussed the work of one of the great photographers of our time. As a backdrop to the conversation, there was a large blow-up of one of his creations—a beautiful sculptured mountain with three unadorned telephone poles in the foreground. To the untrained eye it is merely three poles in front of a hill. In fact, it is a dramatic and creative composition. As the panel was discussing the merits of the photograph, the interviewer asked, "Couldn't anybody take a camera, go out there and take the same picture?" "No, no, nobody else could do it," one of the critics said. "Why not?" asked the interviewer. "Because nobody else would see it," the critic replied.

This is the genius of the Possibility Thinker. He sees in everything around him what others fail to see.

He listens to an idea and says: "That could be very innovative." Others say, "We never did it that way before."

He listens to a big dreamer and says, "He's a comer. I'll keep an eye on him." Others say: "He's just dreaming. It will never happen."

He faces a problem and says: "I will make this problem

my opportunity." Others say: "I can't handle it. I better accept defeat gracefully."

The Apostle Paul was a Possibility Thinker. He had been shipwrecked on his way to prison, but he was not defeated. "I can do all things through God who strengthens me," he said, and on the island of Malta in the Mediterranean, where he and the ship's crew and passengers were taken after the storm destroyed the vessel, he immediately seized the opportunity to tell the islanders about the miraculous, wonder-working power of God.

Now that's the Possibility Perspective. Paul had been shipwrecked, *but* he still had his opportunity, and he made the most of it. That attitude is common with all Possibility Thinkers. They know the power of the positive *but*. "I have lost my husband," a woman wrote to me, and then added, *"but* I still have my children." "I lost a lot of money in the stock market," another person said, *"but* I still have my home."

It works the other way, too. "I hear there was a hail storm in Ohio," I said to someone, "Has it hit you?" "Not yet," he replied. Incredible! The poor fellow was so inflicted with the negative *but,* that he was just waiting for trouble to happen.

The Possibility Perspective at Work

Here's how Possibility Thinkers work. When an idea strikes, they:

- *Try* it. They examine it by asking a basic question. "Would this fill a need, heal a hurt, solve a problem or help a person?" If the answer is yes, they:

- *Eye* it. They visualize the concept. They paint it vividly in their imagination, making it beautiful as well as helpful. Then they:
- *Buy* it. They make a commitment to move ahead, taking an option out on the opportunity before it is lost to fast-moving time, or to faster-moving people. Next, they:
- *Fly* it. Like a boy with a kite, they run the idea up, where it soon catches wind. Once off the ground, support soon comes from unexpected sources. Now they:
- *Tie* it. Up and down. They know that dreams have an inclination to drift away when inevitable frustration moves in. So they develop a possibility attitude toward every frustration, difficulty, obstacle, and problem. They simply will not accept defeat. They never give up because they make a habit out of turning negatives into positives.

Turning negatives into positives! How is it done? Again, it's a matter of a Possibility Perspective. Once a father bragged to his son about what a great hunter he was. The son joined his father on the next hunting trip to see for himself. They sat in the duck blind for a time when one lonely waterfowl winged its way through the sky. The father took aim, fired, and missed. "Son," he said, "You have just witnessed a miracle. There flies a dead duck."

Then there was the son who bragged to his dad about what a great hitter he was. "Show me," his dad said. So the youngster threw a ball in the air and swung at it with his bat. He missed. "Strike one," said the father. He did it again. "Strike two," laughed the father. And again. "Strike three." "Boy I am really a great pitcher," said the lad.

Possibility Thinkers become addicted to such mental attitudes. They simply don't know what losing is. Every problem becomes a profitable project. Every obstacle becomes an opportunity. Defeats inspire greater feats. In everything they do, they demonstrate that losers can become winners, too.

In contrast, Impossibility Thinkers are led by a powerful enemy deep within them, an inner force that holds them back, a voice that warns them not to move ahead, a voice that shouts out winsome promises of comfort if they will shrink from the risky challenges of an untested and unexplored adventure. They turn their lives over to this invisible inner dictator and become guilty of bumpy, dumpy, slumpy, lumpy thinking. What do I mean?

- *Bumpy Thinking.* The bump in the road looms as a mountain in the mind of the Impossibility Thinker. He's stopped.
- *Dumpy Thinking.* The Impossibility Thinker collects negative memories. His mind becomes a dumping ground of hurts, rejections, setbacks, and failures. He's defeated.
- *Slumpy Thinking.* When business is good, the Impossibility Thinker says, "It can't last." When it's bad, he says, "We haven't seen the worst yet." He expects slumps, so he gets slumps, and is therefore convinced that his impossibility thinking is evidence of his prophetic brilliance. So a habit is turned into a character.
- *Lumpy Thinking.* The Impossibility Thinker gets his value systems mixed up so that he no longer thinks straight. He's confused. So he puts off making a decision until "things clear up," which more often than not means that he decides to move only after the opportunity is past.

By contrast, a Possibility Thinker makes bold decisions. Because his value system is clear, decision-making is dealt with responsibly, swiftly, and confidently. Most significantly, he doesn't surrender leadership to problems, real or imaginary, certain or uncertain. *He makes the right decision because it is the right decision, not because he is sure of success.* Even when he experiences reverses, he does not hesitate. He turns reverses into a power-generating backswing. Possibilities, not problems, command the leadership of his life. His daring exploits attract the attention of great people who (if impressed with the Possibility Thinker's integrity, which matches his courage) move to his side and offer help. No wonder Possibility Thinkers succeed. And no wonder that Impossibility Thinkers fail. They attract no attention, fail to impress important people who can help them, and are left to fail alone.

Don't Confuse Your Dreams with Your Problems

Now I want to share with you another important secret. The Possibility Perspective does not mix the problem-solving phase with the decision-making phase. The energy and creativity needed to solve problems is only released in minds that are unconditionally committed to making right decisions. The Possibility Perspective assumes that if the idea or cause is right, then somehow every problem will be solved. There are, of course, problems connected with every great idea. But problem-solving ideas will never be conceived until the right and risky decisions are made.

Look what might have happened if Moses, listening to the groaning of 400,000 Hebrews in Egypt, had said, "All right,

I know you want to get out of here. I'll decide to lead you just as soon as I figure out how to cross the sea that stands between us and the Promised Land. It's too wide to swim and too deep to wade. And I don't imagine I could get all 400,000 of you moving without Pharaoh finding out that something is happening. And I'm not about to get us caught between his army and the sea."

If Moses had tried to solve the problem before deciding to lead the people, he would have never made the decision to move ahead. Instead, he made the decision and actually led the people before he had the problem solved. And what happened? As Pharaoh's army pursued them to the sea, the waters parted and the people crossed in safety. The lesson? Possibility Thinkers first make the right decision. Only after the right decision is made is every ounce of energy concentrated on problem-solving. Here, very simply, is how history is shaped. *Great people are ordinary people who make extraordinary decisions.* Often they do so because they don't know it can't be done.

An internationally famous mathematician shared this story about himself with me. It happened when he was a senior at Stanford University. He came to class late one day, after the professor had handed out the test assignment. There were also two problems on the chalkboard, not included on the mimeographed test sheet. After an hour he had completed the test, but still had not solved the two problems on the board. After awhile, he asked the professor if it was all right to take those problems home and work on them there.

"Those two problems were really tough," he reported to me. "I worked on them for three days. The one I never did solve. The other one I did, but I never worked on anything so hard in all my life. So I finally turned my paper in on a Friday morning with that one problem left unsolved.

"Early Sunday morning," the man continued, "my professor knocked on my door. He was flushed and excited and showed me a paper he planned to read at a meeting of the International Mathematics Society. Boy, was I surprised. What the paper told about was how I had solved an unsolvable problem."

"You came to class late," the professor explained, "and didn't know that I had put those two problems on the board to illustrate that there are some problems that couldn't be solved. Not even by Einstein. But you didn't know that. And you solved one anyway."

"That resulted in a professorship at the University of California, at Berkeley," my friend said, adding, "Suppose I had heard the professor say that these were unsolvable problems? Do you think I would have ever solved that one?"

The Possibility Perspective works anywhere. Mother Teresa used it in India in her famous "home of the dying." Determined that dying people deserve to be treated with dignity, she left the security of the convent with only a coin in her pocket, and went into the streets of Calcutta looking for dying people. She dragged their dying bodies into a temple that had been offered to her by the city—a deserted and dirty place, which she cleaned up and put to use. There she loved and cared for the dying people until they passed away. "Everybody at least deserves to have somebody love them while they are dying," she said.

But then an amazing thing began to happen. Even though Sister Teresa takes only terminal cases, when they come there they feel the love of Christ and they get hope—and many stop dying! So one of the nurses said to me when I visited there. "We are going to have to change the name of this place from the Home of the Dying to the Home of the Living."

It works in New York City, too. On a visit there, I hailed a cab. The driver of this particular cab was unforgettable. He had a gold ring hanging from his nostril. I guess I stared at him before I got in his vehicle. He suddenly got excited, rolled down his window, and said, "Dr. Schuller, Hour of Power."

That settled it. I leaped with enthusiasm into the back seat. I wanted to hear his story.

"Dr. Schuller," he said, "you changed my life. We watch you on television every Sunday from my tiny little place in Harlem. You keep saying, 'Possibility Thinking,' But I said, 'That's fine for you to say. You're white and live in Southern California. I'm black, live in Harlem, and am on welfare.' My wife heard my negative remarks and said, 'See, you are doing just what Dr. Schuller says makes you a failure. Why don't you practice what he is telling you?'

"'But I'm black, and I can't get a job. There's nothing I can do.'

"But she persisted, made me really list all the possibilities. 'You can drive a car,' she said. 'Why not get a job driving a cab?' I said, 'Yeah, but the first thing they will ask is what color I am, and that will finish me.' She really nagged me, so to shut her up, I called this cab company, and the first question they asked me was, 'What color are you?' I was about to hang up when the voice said, 'If you are black, we can use you. We need black drivers. Whites are afraid to drive in Harlem.'"

The reason the Possibility Perspective works anywhere is because it inspires people to think bigger than they have ever thought before. That's the secret of success. *Think Bigger!* Think bigger than anyone else in your community, your club, or your profession.

It really works!

A young man called me one day, all the way from Ireland. "Dr. Schuller," the caller said, "I had this idea that I should call you. Somebody gave me a copy of your book *Move Ahead with Possibility Thinking.* I am the pastor of a struggling church, and I want you to know that the book really inspired me."

He then told how his congregation had gone ahead and bought twelve acres of land near a freeway interchange in Belfast, and how he had started to hold services in the center of the city and how both Catholics and Protestants were coming.

"We have rented the largest auditorium in Belfast for Easter, and we are going to fill it," he said. I could tell that he meant it. "I don't have money to waste," he continued, "but I had this strong feeling that I should call you, that you would say something to help me, because I can't find a single Possibility Thinker in all of Northern Ireland. You don't know the mental climate here. It's terrible, with the bombing and the terrorism. Just say something to me."

I wasn't sure what to say, so I assured him he had a great idea and urged him to stick with it. Then I said, "It would be great if you could come to one of our Institutes for Successful Church Leadership." "That's a great idea," he said, "I'll have to pray about it." (I conduct these five-day institutes four times a year in Garden Grove, California.)

A short time later I mentioned this call to one of our laymen, who had previously sponsored a couple of pastors to the Institute. "It would be great," I said, "if we could bring this young man from Ireland to attend the Institute, if we can find someone to pick up his air fare." I got no further in the conversation than that. "You know, Dr. Schuller," he said, "For two weeks I have been bothered about the troubles in Ireland. And I have been praying, asking God if there isn't something our church can do. I'll pick up the tab. Call him right back and tell him to come." Imagine the Irishman's surprise when he learned that he was to be given a free round trip from Ireland to the United States. He came, and today he has one of the most inspiring ministries in the world.

Let me repeat right here something I have said before, and will say again: *The Possibility Perspective holds that Positive Ideas come from God, and are, therefore, possible!* God has only one way to get into your life and mine, and that's through the brain or through the emotion. He gives you an idea. And if that idea passes the test (Will it be great for God? Will it help people? Is anybody else doing the job?) then you know it comes from God. And if that idea is also impossible, that's further evidence it came from God. You didn't just dream it up. He gave it to you. And when you respond to a big positive idea, you give God a chance to work a miracle in your life.

Possibility Perspective demands Big Thinking—so big that it often requires large amounts of patience. Patience to hold on through tough times, through the perspiration phase—a phase that all success projects go through. This is God's way of making sure that we will be made so permanently humble that he can trust us with the big success he wants to give us.

I know how difficult this waiting time can be. I had this Big Dream of a dynamic church with a beautiful building, and of the Tower of Hope with a twenty-four-hour live telephone counseling ministry. I dreamed of a staff of eight ministers, of 1000 laypeople doing the teaching, the counseling, and the work. But my dream was stalled. All the Possibility Thinking I could muster left me trapped in a corner. For two years God tested me, to make sure he could trust me, before he began to give me the success he was planning. That was easy for God to do, to keep me humble. His biggest task was to keep me believing bigger and better and more beautifully than I had ever thought before. There are, I had to learn, no mammoth tasks, only little minds.

How the Possibility Perspective Unfolds

Because Possibility Thinkers believe that their great ideas come from God, they treat them carefully – reverently and prayerfully. Possibility Ideas are a priceless gift and, like newborn infants, must be protected from exposure to negative "carriers of a mental virus," which could prove fatal to the new idea, still too young to live without strong, affectionate, sterilized support. Protect the ideas. Nourish them and feed them. Give them a chance to live and grow. Guide, control, restrain, encourage them, and someday they will surprise everyone with their greatness.

The Possibility Perspective unfolds first by treating all positive ideas carefully and by dreaming dreams prayerfully. Here are four rules to follow as you start dreaming your own dreams:

1. Never discard or ignore any beautiful idea just because it is impossible. Almost all of God's ideas seem impossible when they first come to our minds. That's God's way of testing us.
2. Never reject an exciting idea because it's ego fulfilling as well as society serving. We all need ego fulfillment. "It is God at work in you, giving you the will and the power to achieve his purposes" (Phil. 2:13).
3. Never oppose a good idea because there's something wrong with it. There is no such thing as a perfect idea. There is something wrong with every good idea. You expect this, and you isolate, insulate, neutralize, or sublimate the negative aspect.
4. Never use a problem as an excuse for quitting. Assume that God has a purpose for the problem. Sit tight. Hold fast. Keep on moving!

As the Possibility Perspective further unfolds, it never loses sight of five basic positive principles:

1. Let your values guide you. You will not violate your moral or ethical values.
2. The problems you face, actual or potential, may delay or detour but will not defeat you.
3. Money, time, energy, brainpower will not even be considered at the "brain-storming" stage. You assume all this is manageable later—somehow, some way, sometime.
4. The size of your faith in God alone will set the ceilings and boundaries to your dream.
5. You are willing to pay any price—dollars, time, dedication—to accomplish whatever dream God puts in your mind.

Finally, the unfolding Possibility Perspective dictates that you follow three steps as you try to climb the ladder to Super-success:

1. Get in tune with God's Holy Spirit. He becomes the source of your idea.
2. Get in touch with God's helpers. He has experts in every field. He puts the dreams and the doers together to make a team.
3. Get in time with God's calendar. You may have to move fast—very fast! Or you may have to wait—weeks, months, years. Just remember that God's delays are not God's denials.

Once I wanted something from the safe deposit box we keep in our home. But the key was misplaced, so I took the box to a locksmith to see if he could find a way to open it. But he couldn't find another key, so he handed it back to me. As he did this, his fingers got under the lid. Amazing! The lid lifted up. It was unlocked all the time. And there, right on the top, inside the box was the key.

God has a beautiful life planned for you and the key is inside of you—the key is the Possibility Perspective. To start moving, remember that nobody puts you down more than the person who set your goals for you.

God can't perform a miracle until you have committed yourself to something that is humanly impossible. Just remember, an impossibility is nothing more than a big idea that hits a mind that has to think bigger. With us it is impossible, but with God all things are possible.

5 Succeed Where You Have Failed Before

If you have failed in your marriage, your interpersonal relationships, your academic pursuits, in maintaining your own physical or spiritual health, you can still be a winner. Losers can be winners, too.

I want you to imagine this picture in your mind's eye. I want you to visualize racers running around a track. There is one person leading the race, with others following close behind. But there is one person trailing far in the rear. Imagine yourself as the last person in the race, with a great space between you and the others who are leading and running to win. Suddenly the announcer says, "The man who is trailing is closing the gap!" The crowd is on its feet. As they draw near to the wire, the man in last place is cutting to the outside. The announcer yells, "It's a photo finish!" *You won!* It's the upset of the day.

History is filled with stories of upsets when all computer predictions and expert projections are thrown to the winds. Your life can be an inspiring upset story, too.

Ed Gibson flunked first and fourth grades. But he went on to become an astronaut.

Abraham Lincoln ran for office seven times and was defeated every time. He still went on to become the president of the United States.

Dr. Victor Frankl was excluded from the Psychiatric Society in Vienna, Austria. He went on to become one of the most prominent and respected psychiatrists in the world today.

Bobby Kennedy flunked first grade. He went on to become attorney general of the United States.

Then there's Richard Sutton. His is an amazing story. When he was a small boy he met Herbert Hoover. Hoover was taken by the lad and suggested that when he grew up he should become a lawyer and go to Stanford University. He even promised to help. The years passed, and when the lad graduated from high school, he wrote Mr. Hoover, reminding him of that chance meeting years before. Hoover kept his promises and when the young man graduated from law school, Hoover urged him to go back to his native Hawaii and run for office as a Republican. The young man did that and lost. "Keep running until you win," Mr. Hoover urged. But that was not a simple formula for success. Hawaii's population is heavily Democratic, a fact that made the challenge harder. But no matter, he kept running anyway. Seven, eight, nine, ten, eleven times. Always he lost. Then came November 1974, and he decided to run again. In Hawaii, like most states, it was a Democratic sweep. But miracles do happen, and this fellow won.

Richard Sutton finally became a legislator for the state of Hawaii at fifty-six years of age, after eleven defeats. Quitters never win and winners never quit. So keep running until you win.

Turn Your Thinking Around – and Win

Losers become winners when they remodel their thinking. The Apostle Paul, in the Bible, gives us this wise advice: "Do not be conformed to this world but be transformed by the renewal of your mind." The "world," in its Biblical usage, refers to that total aggregation of human beings who are unrelated to God. Such people are essentially skeptical, negative-thinking, cynical people. They distrust themselves, they distrust others, and they distrust God.

No, do not be conformed to the world, but "be transformed by the renewal of your minds." There is the key to succeeding where you have always failed before.

If you want to start succeeding and stop failing, take note of these seven stumbling blocks to success. I have studied the patterns of chronic losers and habitual underachievers and have noticed that they are persistently plagued by them. Check them and in the process reconstruct your own minds.

1. BLIGHTS

The loser is often a person who has developed a self-image of imperfectionism when he was small, and he carries the effects of this "ism" over into adult life. When you were two or three years of age you may have thought of your parents as being perfect. You could never achieve their level of goodness, or wisdom. Because you came to believe they were perfect, you also felt that you were not as good a person as they were. Comparing yourself against your infantile impression of them gave you a sense of inferiority that allowed you to say to yourself, "I don't deserve to succeed. I'm not good enough." This can be the beginning of the will to fail. Even though you claim you want to succeed, at the deepest level of your life, you actually will to fail because you really don't think you deserve to win.

So people deliberately plan to fail. Failure doesn't happen accidentally. It is designed, planned, and shaped in advance. It may be conscious or subliminal. Even when there is every appearance of success, some people feel that their lives are a failure down deep within themselves because they cannot compete with their parents.

One day an old man, eighty-two years of age, came to talk with me. He was a very successful and even famous man. He came, at a time near the end of his life, to say that even after all his achievements he felt he was not half the man his father was.

"My Scottish father was a poor farmer, but he could pray the most beautiful prayers in church and in the home. By comparison I feel I am a failure," he said. I felt sorry for him as he poured his lifelong anxiety out to me.

He then told how he, himself, had left Scotland as a youth, and had come to America. Starting out without a nickel to his name, he became one of California's most successful homebuilders. "But I never was the man my father was," he lamented.

"Look," I said, "Tens of thousands of people today live in beautiful homes in Southern California because you built these houses. You made it possible for hundreds of thousands of people to have paychecks and they were able to go home and buy food for their children. There are tens of thousands of Christmas trees this year at the hearthsides that you built. Think of all the people, the homes, and the families that have shelter and food and a little savings account because of your life's work." His face brightened, became radiant. I added, "Your father was good at offering prayers, but you have been great at answering them."

He looked at me in amazement. He had never seen it that way before. "That helps, that really helps," he said.

Remodel your thinking by eliminating the tendency to put yourself down because you are not perfect.

2. FRIGHTS

The fear of failure or fear of competition is another common mental malady that affects the steady loser.

Some people deliberately fail because the only way they know how to win is to keep on losing. By losing, they say to their friends, "I told you I couldn't do it," which, you see, is in itself a form of winning. "See, I told you that it would come out this way. Look how smart I am!"

This, too, has some very curious aspects. The noted psychiatrist, Dr. Robert Steinberg, has explained that a child of four already feels himself in competition with his father. Even at that young age, he contends, a child can fear success—may actually fear that if he succeeds he will have to compete with his father. That fear may continue on into later life and sub-

consciously express itself in a neurotic pattern that spells continuous failure.

Mildred Newman and Bernard Berkowitz, in their book
How to Be Awake and Alive, tell of a young man they call
"Chuck," who showed promise as an actor. But every time
Chuck was offered a part in a play or movie, he got upset
and quarrelled with the producer over some small detail, until
the whole opportunity fizzled out. In counseling, Dr. Berkowitz
suggested that Chuck imagine that he was in his hometown,
that his name was on the marquee of the local theater, and
that his parents were walking across the street, seeing his name
in lights.

At this suggestion, Chuck exploded. "No! No!" he shouted,
"They don't deserve it! They don't deserve to see me a success." Right there, Chuck's "will-to-fail" was exposed. On a
subliminal level he hated his father and mother so intensely
that he would never give them the satisfaction of his own success. He wanted to fail in order to punish them.

Still others avoid success because they really suspect success. I once met a minister who was failing because he believed that to strive for success was a lack of humility. "The
very opposite is the truth," I advised him. "To strive to succeed calls for great humility. You have to be humble enough
to risk the embarrassment of possible failure."

But for some people this is very hard to see. I am thinking
of people whose minds have been warped by an irresponsible fundamentalism, the kind of religious belief that says, "God
means for you to suffer. God means for you to fail. If you
are interested in success, you just aren't spiritual; that's a
worldly goal." I say without qualification that this flight from
success is a basic distortion of Christianity. Positive religion

teaches that every person's duty is to glorify God. Success, as we have defined it—building self-esteem in yourself and in others through sincere service—is a sure road to the kind of living that glorifies God.

3. FIGHTS

In the English movie, *The Loneliness of the Long Distance Runner*, a young man is motivated by his headmaster to excel as a runner. He gradually improves his skills until it looks as though he is going to be the greatest runner in England.

Shortly before the championship race, the headmaster who also was his coach and who had befriended him all along, betrayed him. When it came time for the big race, the runner moved out ahead of his competition, but as he approached the wire he suddenly stopped in his tracks, put his arms across his chest and just stood there while the other runners passed him by. He deliberately chose to fail. Why?

We get the answer in the movie. The runner, standing as still as a post, glares at the headmaster in rage and says, "I got even with you!" Is the will to fail a manipulative attempt to lash back at someone who has hurt you? We fail because we want to get even, and thereby show other people up.

As you remodel your mind, analyze your deepest feelings. Be sure you are not using your failures as a means to vent your hostility and resentment.

4. NIGHTS

Maybe it's the dark times in your past—the times when you were hurt or disillusioned—that are holding you back. Or maybe it's your feelings of guilt that cause you to fail over and over again. Failure is tragic business because it becomes so repeatable. It becomes a habit to which we become adjusted. Some people cultivate that habit by allowing their guilt to contribute to their will to fail. For by failing they believe they can expiate their sins and guilt. It's incredible what lengths people will go to try to earn their own salvation. Some people try to give money to the poor. But more of us, I believe, try to buy our salvation by punishing ourselves – by deliberately failing, so that the effect is much the same as that of holy men of India who sit on beds of nails.

Although such deep stirrings of an anguished soul are difficult to calm, it is helpful if we get a different perspective on failure. We have to understand failure for what it is.

- Failure doesn't mean you'll never make it. It does mean you have to do it differently.
- Failure doesn't mean you don't have it. It does mean you have to make some deep changes.
- Failure doesn't mean you'll never succeed. It does mean it will take longer.
- Failure doesn't mean you're a fool to try again. It does mean you have the courage to keep making noble commitments and great resolutions.
- Failure doesn't mean God doesn't answer prayers. It does mean that God has a better idea.*

*Robert H. Schuller, *You Can Become the Person You Want to Be* (New York: Hawthorn, 1973), p. 73.

5. LIGHTS

Some people achieve a small success and then they are satisfied. They want to prove something to themselves, and when they succeed, they quit. They are like mountain climbers who are satisfied when they have reached the first high ridge, while the top of the mountain rises above them. They climb the first rung of the ladder of their ultimate potential and then stop. If the night of dark experiences holds some people back, the light of success holds others. Dr. Frankl, the noted Viennese psychiatrist, put it forcefully when he said, "The *is* must never catch up with the *ought*."

I know many people like that. They have had their small victories—just enough success to prove to themselves that they are worthy people, and then they start relaxing. They are like people who quit pedaling a bicycle. They haven't learned that if you stop pedaling, you tip over. You have to keep moving ahead or you die. Stop and you either begin to decay or go backward. Self-esteem, like manna, cannot be stored without spoiling on the shelf.

Some people stop short of the goals because they really don't feel a need to succeed. They are so secure inwardly, so self-assured, that they don't need to prove anything to themselves or to other people. So they don't strive. But to such people, let me say, it's not a question of whether you *feel* the need to succeed. The question is, what does God want you to achieve? What does God expect of you? What are the crying needs in your community that call for your help?

6. SIGHTS

Some people hold themselves back because they think they are too short, too tall, too old, too poor. But almost always the problem is not with being "too anything." The solution is to think bigger and deeper. Even to try harder. You have to set your sights higher.

Perhaps you know the story of the fisherman who always threw the biggest fish he caught back into the lake. The only ones he kept were ten inches long or less. "Why are you doing that?" a curious bystander asked. "Well," said the fisherman, "my frying pan is only ten inches across."

All of us are guilty of "ten-inch" thinking. The biggest idea that ever came into your mind—you threw away! For you were sure it was impossible.

We don't think big enough, and so we fail. We content ourselves with solving all the little problems, but then we let the big ones get us down. Meanwhile we let our little achievements get swallowed up by the bigger problems—because we don't think big enough to meet the challenge that overwhelms us.

7. FLIGHTS

Some people fail to succeed because they are not willing to make a deep enough commitment. Under the pressure of problems they collapse, quit, and "take flight."

You can succeed if you develop an inner strength to commit yourself completely to your marriage, your interpersonal relationships, your academic pursuits, your career. Stop flying, settle down. Stay with it. A flighty person is always changing his mind, is shiftless, nervous, not in control of his thinking. But a committed person is calm and capable of making correct decisions quickly because he knows exactly what he wants to achieve. He welcomes constructive criticism and is willing to face his faults. Nobody ever wins unless he looks at himself constructively, positively and self-critically to find the areas where improvement is possible. When a person gets the courage to admit the need for help, he begins to study and to learn.

Rise Stevens, one of the greatest sopranos of all time, tells how she prepared for years to win a competitive prize giving her an opportunity to sing on a national radio network. She hired a coach and borrowed thousands of dollars to pay for her lessons. In competition, she made it all the way to the semifinals. After her performance, she waited for the judges' decision. Then the phone rang with the sad news. "I'm sorry to tell you that you were not selected. I thought your voice was best, but the other judges felt your competitor had more experience," said the chief judge.

Miss Stevens was in tears. At the moment it seemed that the bottom had dropped out of everything. She had risked all she had and now she had nothing. Her coach looked at her and for a time said nothing. Then, slowly, he got out of his chair, walked over to her, and said, "Miss Stevens, all I can say is, have the courage to face your faults. Your next lesson will be at two o'clock this afternoon." And that was the beginning of her great success. She was soon off on a European tour and when she returned she was heralded for her great achievements.

By now I trust you have checked your mental habits and are ready to remodel your thinking from a "loser mind-set" to a "winner mind-set." Now believe, confidently, courageously, unswervingly that with the help of God you have the turnaround power you need to succeed where you have failed before.

Briefly, by using the letters S–U–C–C–E–S–S, let's review the steps:

S – SELECT YOUR GOAL

If you don't know what you want to hit, don't be surprised if you miss the mark. When you find a person who has one clear goal that he wants to accomplish with all his being, and he knows it is God's will for him, you might as well get out of his way.

Select a goal, prayerfully, before God, that has as its major human value service to others. If fame or fortune is your objective, you may succeed, but you may lose your own soul in winning.

Begin by looking for a person who needs help, somebody with problems, and plan to do something to help solve those problems. Before you know it, you will have customers gravitating to you. You will have to hire others to help those coming to you for help. It's a fact! If you are sincerely interested in helping people, you may wind up becoming wealthy someday. But wealth should always be a by-product and never your objective.

U – UNLOCK THE POTENTIAL
THAT IS STILL IMPRISONED WITHIN YOU

There is no one who doesn't have undiscovered talent. I don't care how old or young you are.

Some of you may be relaxing because you are retired. You are sixty-five, seventy, or even eighty years old. You would like to relax and take it easy. Or you may think no one needs you anymore. The truth is everyone can do something to help someone. God does not expect you to sit back in a chair and take a vacation for the rest of your life. So long as you live, God wants you to be productive, to be creative, to use your energy for his glory. Just because you don't have a paycheck is no excuse for just vegetating.

The most brilliant person in the world uses only about 10 percent of his brain cells. The other 90 percent remain unused, but alive. The untapped power within you is like the universe around us – the almost limitless universe that we haven't seen as yet, even with the use of power telescopes.

A maid who worked in the studio of a famous sculptor would come each evening to sweep up the trimmings. One day she saw a form begin to emerge out of the marble. It looked like the head of a man. Then she saw a face. The next night the whole head. Finally, one night she came just as the artist was ready to leave, and she saw for the first time the fully sculptured form. "Why, that's Abraham Lincoln," she cried to the artist. "How did you know Mr. Lincoln was in there?"

God sees more inside of you than you can imagine. Let

God unlock the hidden possibilities. Let your greatness out. Select your goal. Then unlock your potential.

C – COMMIT YOURSELF TO GOD'S PLAN FOR YOUR LIFE

Here are some lines written by H. M. Murray, which I carry with me and read the first thing each morning: "Until one is committed there is hesitancy, a chance to draw back. But the moment one definitely commits oneself, then God moves too, and a whole stream of events erupts. . . . All manner of unforeseen incidents, meetings, persons and material assistance which no man could have dreamt come his way and begin to flow toward him."

Commit yourself. Quit thinking, "if," "maybe," "might," "probably I will." All of these hold you back. Hesitancy blocks the flow of power, but total commitment releases a multitude of mysterious gifts that come to you from unbelievable and unknown powers. There is nothing you cannot do if God wants you to do it.

Select your goal. Unlock your potential. Then commit yourself. Make decisions before you see solutions to the problems. That's what commitment really means.

C – CHART YOUR COURSE

There is a way in which you can accomplish the impossible. Begin now by making a plan. Instead of complaining, make a list from one to ten on a sheet of paper and let your imagination run wild. List ten ways in which you think you might accomplish something everyone else knows is impossible. Put those ideas down where you won't forget them. Don't let anyone talk you out of them. What you are doing now is playing a game, a deadly serious game! Try it and you will see that you can dream of ten ways to accomplish the impossible. That's the starting point for charting a course.

No complaining that it can't be done is allowed in this game. That is the only rule. A mother once told her complaining daughter what all of us need to hear: "Listen, daughter," she said, "I gave you life, I gave you love, I gave you faith, I gave you shelter, food, and clothing, but that's all I can give you. Now do something with it, and stop complaining."

Do something with it. Chart your course.

E – EXPECT PROBLEMS

As you pursue your plans, expect difficulties. But know in advance that every problem provides an experience from which you can learn. Problems stretch our minds. Nobody would ever think bigger if they didn't face challenging problems. So expect them and welcome them.

S – STAND FIRM ON YOUR COMMITMENT

Persistence and resolute determination are the next steps on the road to success. Stand firm for honesty and integrity. Never do anything dishonest. Never be a phony, it will come out, and when it does, you are finished.

To you young people, a word of advice. Believe in the old-time morality. It isn't old for nothing. It's classical; it has passed the test of time. So stand firm. When you leave the shelter

of your home and church, you will be challenged to throw
away your old-fashioned morality. But that's the devil's game.
It's the way of failure. Stand firm! Your character is absolutely
essential for becoming a successful person. Moral steadfast-
ness produces power. Tremendous emotional energy and
physical stamina are released by moral discipline. It is one
of the keys to prolonged youthfulness. You stay young only
as long as you live up to your youthful ideals. Just as soon
as you give up a youthful ideal, you may not be aware of it,
but you are taking a giant step into old age.

H. G. Wells discovered this truth also, which he drama-
tized in one of his plays about a highly idealistic youth who
looked like a breath of springtime. He had great visions and
dreams. But along the way he lost them. Soon he was drinking more than he should, and then he became involved in
an adulterous affair.

The years pass swiftly and at the end of the play we see
him as an old man. In the last scene the stage is empty and
dark. The curtains are drawn, and onto the stage the once
fresh and bright young man, now wrinkled and bent over
with age, turns to his audience. He says he has been looking
for the North Star, the star he once spotted as a Boy Scout.
He hasn't seen it for years, and now he can't find it. Suddenly
he shakes and trembles, throws out his arms and says, "Oh
God, give me my ideals back! Maybe I'll be young again." And
the curtain drops.

Remember, you will not fail until you decide to fail yourself. No person is a loser unless he quits. Stand firm.

Now recheck those letters S–U–C–C–E–S–S. They truly tell
you how to stop losing and start winning. Are you ready for
the last guidepost?

S – SURRENDER EVERYTHING YOU ARE AND EVERYTHING YOU HOPE TO BE TO JESUS CHRIST

I don't know how much you want climb in life, or how far you will go, but I can tell you this. When the curtain drops, and you meet your Lord, the only thing that will count then is: Did you live and succeed for the purpose of helping God and his children? That's the final tabulation, the ultimate accounting of your success.

Aaron Burr was one of the greatest men in American history, and at the same time one of the most ignoble. His name lives in infamy as a traitor to our land. He was to die a disgraceful and dishonorable person.

The turning point in his life came when he was a student at Princeton University. It was during a "religious emphasis week" that a speaker challenged every person to give his life to Christ. Aaron Burr stayed up late that night, pacing the room where he lived. He faced the ultimate question: should he give his life to Jesus Christ or not? In the early morning hours he made his decision. Suddenly, he flung open the shutters of his dormitory and called out into the darkness: "Good-bye, Jesus Christ!" And he slammed the shutters shut.

I have no doubt that the reason my life has been successful is because I, as a young man, threw open the window of my life to say, "Come in, Jesus Christ. I have but one life to live and I don't want to blow it. If you are running my life, I'll trust your leadership. Take my life and make it great. Between the two of us, we can do that."

That's the choice before you now. Nobody and nothing can stop you from becoming what God wants you to be. Nobody, but *You!*

6 Goal-Setting – First Rule of Leadership

Check into the lives of the Supersuccessful People, institutions, and businesses, and what single positive quality stands out? I can answer that question with a single word: *Leadership*. And what is leadership? It is the force that sets the goals in individual and institutional life.

You face a choice. You can either live your life marked by constant crisis intervention or by creative leadership. Creative leadership envisions opportunities and moves ahead to capture the moment, mold it, and make it great. The creative leader also envisions potential problems and then directs personal or public events to avoid them, prevent them, defend against them; or he develops plans to turn problems into creative opportunities. Problems are never problems if you are prepared for them with creative leadership. The life marked by creative leadership is always building an ever-broadening power base. It is not an easy way to live, but it is the only constructive way.

Not easy at all! The price is hard work, tough thinking, risky planning, daring decision-making and honest promoting. Mark this and note it well. Nobody can be a supersuccess unless he is prepared to be a promoter. He has to sell himself to himself first of all.

An honest, effective leader is a dynamic promoter. He sells solutions to problems to people who need to buy these solutions, but don't know it. Few tasks are more difficult than convincing people that they should spend money ahead of time. But the creative leader sees the problem down the road. He tries to communicate to those whose support and endorsement he needs the knowledge that a problem is coming up, that it will not go away by ignoring it, that it will get worse by waiting longer, and that delays will increase the cost of the inevitable solution.

The price of creative leadership is selling your ideas to people. Risky? Of course. There always will be cynics who misinterpret your motives, your methods, or your management styles. The anticipation of criticism is enough of a threat to frighten many people from becoming dynamic leaders. The choice? To become followers. Which often means surrendering leadership of your own future to events over which you then have no control or to persons who desire to manipulate you, or to forces, good or evil, that may strike against you.

As a follower, you are destined to constantly face surprises, most of them negative, that will turn your life into one continuous round of crisis-intervention activity. Because you have surrendered leadership, you have surrendered control of your own life to forces that do not have your best interests at heart. Without control you have lost the power of management.

Without management there will be no planned, goal-directed accomplishments. Waste is the inevitable result. Wasted opportunities, resources, energies, materials, time, pleasure, self-esteem, pride, happiness and success.

Why, then, would anyone surrender leadership? For many reasons. The price of leadership, as we have seen, is exacting. The price of decision-making is a frightening prospect to insecure persons. Then there is also the fear of failure. If you take command and control of your own life by becoming a goal-setting leader, you do, in fact, risk failure. The fear of it and the fear of the results of failure can be devastating. Sigmund Freud thought goals were dangerous because failure to achieve them would be annihilating to self-respect to the point of bringing on neurosis.

Dr. Victor Frankl, the noted Viennese phychiatrist, however, has another view. Failure to achieve your goals, he maintains, is not as dangerous as not having goals. He likes to point to the Old Testament story of how God led the Hebrews in the wilderness with a pillar of fire in front of the people at night and a cloud by day – to pull the people forward. That's what goals do to us. You never catch up with a cloud. You never catch up with the fire. The *is* must never catch up with the *ought*. That's the proper mental attitude. If you set a goal and reach it, and there is no way to expand it, decay and death set in.

Fear of failure, if it leads to abandoning leadership, ends up as ultimate failure. When you surrender your right to leadership, you lose your freedom to choose, which in the end reduces you to becoming an object. That's sure and certain failure. Unless you rise to fill the leadership role God meant for you to take, you will be left to drift in the current of nonnegotiable and irreversible forces over which you have no control.

You have an alternative to such failure. You can develop, grow, and mature into a truly great person. You do this by becoming a goal-setting, goal-directed, goal-motivated, goal-managed, goal-pursuing, goal-inspired, goal-achieving person.

Goals Rise Out of Problems

Remember our definition of success: *Success is building self-esteem in yourself and others through service.* That being true, then goal-setting must rise out of problems that call for solution, needs that must be filled, hurts that cry for healing. Goals so conceived are born in compassion to help people who need help, and for that reason they have the right generic advantage to succeed. So put a soul in your goal. Start by caring for people. It will almost assure success, whether the goal is worked out in respect to personal relationships, business, or industry. Look at where many goals are conceived and you will see why persons and projects fail.

- ● **GOALS MUST NOT RISE OUT OF SELF-CENTERED NEEDS**

The ego needs of decision-making executives are, too often, the birthplace of corporate goals. Now it is necessary for every person to find ego-fulfillment in his work. The need to feel important is natural, normal, and healthy. To deny ego needs is dishonest, unnatural, and falsely pious. But filling the needs of people must become the source of ego-fulfillment. You should never react against a goal because it fills your ego needs, but at the same time do not set your goals only to feed your vanity. You will be safe and sure in this when you discover that your goals are designed to help people. The good feeling that is then produced is ego-fulfillment in its best sense.

Why do great movements in history begin to crest and die? When a movement succeeds, it soon becomes an institution with chief executives and high status, with salary and staffs to match. Right at that point the movement—turned organization—enters a potentially dangerous phase. Now there will be people vying for power and politicking for position. The original goals may become lost and be replaced by goals that rise out of self-serving, self-preserving, and self-promoting egos. Self-centered interests of the leadership people become more important than the unfulfilled needs and unresolved problems of the struggling persons whose needs gave birth to the movement in the first place.

• GOALS MUST NOT RISE OUT OF TRADITION

Legalistically, holding onto tradition is another reason why creative and energetic movements crest. Many goals of individuals and corporate institutions rise out of tradition rather than contemporary human need. This is not to say that tradition is bad. Indeed, just the opposite is true. Tradition is not to be disparaged nor discarded. It is, rather, to be retooled, updated, given new energy, to make sure that it still is touching people where they live today. That point needs emphasis. If anything has become a tradition, you can be sure it has met the needs of people over more than one generation. And if it has survived and successfully bridged the generation gap, you can also be sure that it has a lot of value in it. So before you are tempted to discard some tradition, study the values that gave rise to it and nurtured it in the first place. Then adapt these values and attitudes, learning from the wisdom of earlier generations. That's only good sense. Having done this, you are in a position to modernize the merchanting and marketing of the classic, nonfashionable values so that you become innovative within the tradition rather than destructive of it. We need tradition, but leadership people treat it creatively, always finding new ways to make it work for people in need today.

• GOALS MUST NOT RISE OUT OF POLICY

Another reason why movements, once energetic and creative, fail is that goals tend to rise out of policy rather than people needs. *The lesson we must learn and keep learning is that the needs of people must override corporate policy,* whether in business or government. Policies are needed to make decisions, but policies should always rise out of and be sensitive to human need. When policy forgets people, beware! The spirit of the law will become suffocated by the letter of the law, and the goal will have lost its soul. So put a soul and keep a soul in your goal.

Twenty miles from a hotel where I was to speak at a convention, my car broke down, and that began a chain of events that can only be called frustrating in the extreme. I called a cab, but the driver failed to arrive until forty-five minutes later.

The delay meant reaching the hotel a mere ten minutes before I was to speak—which meant that I could not take time to eat. Since I had had no food all day, I was famished, but no matter! I could always eat later. The speech over, I went in search of the coffee shop, only to find that it had closed at 9:00 P.M., five minutes before I got there. At the front desk of the hotel I learned there was a restaurant three miles down the road, where, if I hurried, I could be served. So I asked a young man in a hotel uniform if he could arrange transportation. No way! He had to stick around in case anyone called from the airport. So I called another taxi. A twenty-minute wait. When I arrived at the restaurant, the drapes were drawn, a few minutes before it was scheduled to close. "Sorry, sir, we're closing," a voice said in response to my pleas. "The chef left a bit early. There's nothing I can do."

So I went to bed hungry, but not before I came to realize again how policy needs often overshadow people needs. If the principle of policies serving people had been ingrained into that hotel, the young man could have and would have quickly run me to the restaurant before it closed. If I had been treated in a helpful manner, I would go back there the next time I were in that city. People needs must override paper policy.

Guidelines to Successful Goal-Setting

From this perspective, let's look at some principles of goal-setting. As we have seen, leadership flounders when goal-setting misfires. A word of wisdom is found in the Bible: "I have set before you life and death, blessing and cursing. Therefore choose life" (Deut. 30:19).

You can choose to be a blessing or a curse to yourself and others. It all depends on the goals you set and how you set them. *And* the exciting thing is that everyone is given the power and the freedom to set personal goals, and thereby become a leader, at least over one's own future. Choose what kind of life you want to live, what you want to accomplish, and what you want to achieve. It all begins with goal-setting.

1. BEGIN WITH POSSIBILITY THINKING

When you set your private goals, your spiritual goals or your professional goals, begin with a Possibility Perspective. Begin with the assumption that if your goal is a beautiful idea, if it is a great thing for God, if it would help people who are suffering, then, of course, there must be a way to achieve it. "With men," said Jesus, "this is impossible, but with God all things are possible." In setting your goals, always assume that somehow, someway impossibilities can be turned around into possibilities.

Rachel Carson, in her book, *Silent Spring,* recalls the dialogue in *Alice in Wonderland* between Alice and the Red Queen. Alice says, "One can't believe impossible things." And the queen says, "I dare say, you haven't had much practice. When I was your age, I always did it for half an hour a day. Why, sometimes I believed in as many as six impossible things before I had breakfast."

"And that," says Rachel Carson, "is a very necessary thing to do and to know. If you start believing impossible things before breakfast, the first thing you know by dinnertime they are not impossible anymore."

2. LET YOUR VALUE SYSTEM GUIDE YOU

Your goals must be compatible or they will be combatible. Unless they are compatible with your own deepest value system, you will have tension, guilt, and anxiety, and you won't be able to succeed. Ask yourself, "What did I believe as a child? What were the deepest, purest, greatest ideas I have ever looked up to?" Perhaps you are cynical, and have separated yourself from those great moral ideals that you once held. In setting your goals, go back to your highest values and ideals and make certain that whatever goals you are setting are compatible with those God-inspired ideals. If they are not, you won't be able to give it all you have.

That's why, ultimately, only the honest people enjoy happy success. For only honest people are genuinely enthusiastic. Dishonest persons develop cold, protective shields around their warm enthusiasm-producing emotions. They have to be careful—or they will expose themselves. Compatible or combatible! Make sure your goals harmonize with your value system. Then you will come to the end of your life with pride behind you, love around you and hope ahead of you.

It has been my joy to know some of the great Christians of our day—E. Stanley Jones, Billy Graham, Norman Vincent Peale. Among these giants is Dr. Bob Pierce, who has to have one of the greatest hearts of our time. Nobody has done more to create orphanages around the world for homeless children than Bob Pierce. In my mind, he is one of the greatest success stories of this century. Recently I took a trip to Mexico to go marlin fishing as a guest of Bob Pierce and his friend and mine, Chuck Walters.

There was a very touching scene for me an hour before we left to come home. Bob Pierce has leukemia and is not expected to live very long. As the hour of our departure came, Bob was lying in his bed, and I was visiting with him. Chuck came in while I was there and said, "I won't say good-bye, Bob. I'm going to believe that you are going to live longer than they think you will."

With a radiance on his face and a serenity that could only come from the presence of Jesus Christ deep within him, Bob said, "You know, I have been talking with my Lord about that, and there just isn't anybody in the world I feel I have to go to and make amends with as I come to the end of my life. And that's a good feeling. I feel beautiful. I really do. I gave my life to Christ and that's the best thing I ever did. Now, in coming to the end, I feel good."

Dr. Bob Pierce comes to the end of his life with pride behind him, love around him and hope ahead of him. It all began in Amoy, China, in 1957, when a missionary there came to Dr. Pierce with an eleven-year-old child. "Take her," she told him. "I have four adopted children of my own, and I can't take another one. You want to be a minister? You want to be a missionary? You want to do something? Here, feed and clothe this little girl." And that was the beginning of what turned out to be Bob Pierce's great ministry. He became the founder of World Vision, which today serves millions of needy persons throughout Asia and the world.

In your goal-setting, begin with problem-solving Possibility Thinking. *With God it is possible.* Then look at your value system. Set your goals in tune with God and his Word, to make sure that if you succeed you will be proud of it. And if you fail you will be proud of your failure, too, because you will know that at least you tried to do something beautiful for God.

3. AIM AT GROWTH IN BOTH QUALITY AND QUANTITY

Avoid the cop-out of saying, "We are not growing in numbers but we are sure growing in quality." If you are really growing in quality, you are going to improve in quantity also, unless you have saturated the international market with your product. This means then, in your goal-setting, you need to look for the growth-restricting areas. Ask yourself, "What is restricting the growth of our company or my own personality?" Leadership looks for growth-restricting obstacles and sets goals in which they are overcome and removed.

To illustrate, our first church in Garden Grove was built on only two acres of land in another part of the city. I could see that the church could grow only so far before it would become nonexpandable. We wouldn't be able to park the cars. So we relocated our church to where it is today, on twenty-two acres, thus allowing us to keep growing.

If the goal is not expandable, then it is expendable. Because the time will come when you are choked and you can't grow. And what will happen then? Dynamic, creative staff people will drift away. Dynamic, creative people can only work in companies, corporations, institutions, and in situations where there is a constant challenge. Replacing them will be the kind of people who don't want to pay the high cost of success, people who want to take it easy. That will be the new leadership. And even a dead fish can float downstream.

So ask yourself if there is some area where you haven't been growing. Is there some department where you haven't been making progress? If your plant or your equipment is limiting your growth, then develop other plants and equipment. If capital is limiting your growth and expansion, then you have to increase your capital. Or, if there are dangerous and debilitating habits and practices within your personal life that are keeping you from growing, then begin at once to overcome these growth-restricting features of your life.

4. STUDY YOUR PREJUDICES, PASSIONS, AND CONCERNS

Chances are you have some blind spots that are holding you back. And we all have them. Your goal-setting efforts should aim at opening up these closed areas. If you feel deeply and passionately on some controversial issue, I suggest that you play a game in which you take the opposite side. Try putting yourself in the other guy's shoes. You may be led into an area of your emotional life where growth and maturity are deeply called for.

5. CHECK THE SUCCESS POTENTIAL
BEFORE YOU SET YOUR GOALS

You can almost always check whether an idea will be a failure or a success before you begin by asking, "Is this idea practical? Will this dream fill a vital human need? Can it excel? Can it inspire? Is it pace-setting? Can your idea be inspirational to others? Can it be packaged in such a way that people will want it? Will it touch them emotionally?" If you are

first with the most, you can't lose unless you don't have the
nerve to move ahead.

6. LET THE SIZE OF YOUR GOD
SET THE LIMITS OF YOUR GOALS

In other words, make your goals big enough for God to fit
in. You can never succeed all by yourself. If you achieve success, it will be because others helped make you successful.
Your responsibility is to set your goals. God will use others
to make them come to pass. That means you begin drawing
support first of all from God. I don't believe any person will
be a happy success without God.

So ask yourself this question. How is your relationship with
God? You dontt want to set goals unless your heart is right
with God. He says to you, "I have set before you life or death,
blessing or curse. Oh, that you would choose life."

7. MAKE YOUR GOALS MEASURABLE

Make your goals specific or else you won't know if you are
succeeding or failing. Then measure your progress. And as
you see success, you will get enthusiastic. You will be in orbit. If your goals are measurable, you will be able to visualize
them. Only when you can inwardly visualize a goal will you
be emotionally turned on–something that is absolutely necessary if you are to be motivated. There's no starting, and for
sure, no succeeding without motivation. So make sure your
goal is specific enough to be translated into a measurable goal
you can visualize.

8. MAKE SURE YOUR GOAL IS REALIZABLE

Your goal needs to be controllable and measurable. To set a goal for "liberating Russia from Communism" is a non-manageable and noncontrollable goal. Possibility Thinking is limited in its goal-setting by this principle. But fear not! This limitation leaves plenty of room for God to give you great and impossible goals and dreams. And these impossible goals can be accomplished—even if you have tried before and failed.

The trick is to get started—for beginning is half done.

7 Self-Starting Power

All Supersuccessful people got their start in a remarkably simple way – by starting. Something stimulated them to take the first step on a trip that was to become a destiny. I can assure you that you will go nowhere until you start, and I can also assure you that you will have a tremendous experience if you will begin. Beginners are enormously satisfying in themselves.

Consider the Joys of Starting

Getting started is the natural reaction to a positive idea. You simply allow a positive idea to have legs and walk – to grow wings and see if it could possibly fly. Anyone, young or old, rich or poor, healthy or handicapped, can respond and react to a positive idea, and begin. Everyone can take the first step.

Starting is not only simple, it is also stimulating. As soon as you commit yourself to beginning, it is amazing what energy, ideas, enthusiasm, and solutions to problems come to you. It is strange. You will find yourself wanting to do what you knew all the time you should do, but didn't care or dare to do.

To create means to cause something to come out of nothing. Nothing creates—energy, drive, insights, enthusiasm, and brilliant ideas—more than the simple stimulating activity of beginning. Starting is so simple that anyone can do it. It's so stimulating that anyone can get a rise out of it. The act of beginning is smart because it often costs little to make the first move, and the possibilities that can come from the single initial act are almost infinite.

Yes, there are infinite possibilities in little beginnings if God is in the idea in the first place. The smartest thing in the world is to give a positive idea a fighting, breathing chance. Not to start, not to begin, not to take the initial step, not to voice your initial support, not to make that little beginning may be to abort an idea God has placed in your mind. And the abortion of a God-implanted idea—a possibility impregnated idea—is unthinkably foolish.

It's Smart to Start

It's smart to start, because this could be your big chance— your once-in-a-lifetime opportunity. You can be absolutely, completely, unquestionably certain that if you do not start you will surely fail. Your only alternative to starting is delaying. To delay until you are sure you will succeed means that you will never make a move—for you can always imagine the possibility of failure. To delay until you have solved all the problems you imagine you may encounter means that you will not make a move either—for you can always imagine new problems as fast as you solve old ones. To delay until you *feel* like starting means you have surrendered your head to the irresponsible, unstable, inconsiderate, unpredictable, and most unpromising whims of your emotions. That's not being smart. It's being stupid. Getting started is so simple, stimulating, smart! And it's the way of success, too. Yes, beginning, taking the first step, is always sure to be, in itself, a great success. Why? Because God put you in this world, not to measure your achievement, but to weigh your faithfulness.

Some of you have never started anything worthwhile in your lives up to this point. You are afraid to do what you think God may want you to do, because you are not sure you can succeed. You are afraid of failure. If you don't achieve what you start out to do, you think your lower level of achievement will be scored a failure. I repeat: God put you in this world, not to measure your achievements but to weigh your faithfulness.

When you start something, even though there is risk involved and you cannot be sure that you will make it, at least you are exercising faith. When you do something that shows you have faith, in that moment you are a success. Anyone who dares to stick his neck out to do something beautiful for God is a successful person because he is showing that he has faith. God will not ultimately measure your achievement. He will measure your faith. God does not expect perfection, but he does expect you to be willing to take a risk for him.

Be sure of this! God rewards only people who demonstrate faith, however small that first act of faith is. "For without faith it is impossible to please God" (Heb. 11:6). Enormous possible returns come to the person who pleases God with that simple, stimulating, smart step of faith. "If you have faith as a grain of mustard seed, you can say to this mountain, move, and nothing will be impossible to you."

To show you how this works, let's roll the calendar back to 1955. An announcement appeared in Eugene, Oregon, newspapers telling of a religious meeting to be held in the town hall. One particular farmer and his wife, Harry and Bertha Holt, read the notice and decided to attend the meeting. That night they saw a film about orphans who were abandoned in Korea after the Korean conflict. The orphans had been fathered by American soldiers and because they were not pure-blooded Korean children, they were rejected by the Korean people. They were, of course, innocent children, helpless, dying, and many of the girls were destined to become prostitutes if they lived.

Bob Pierce, then president of World Vision, led the meeting, and pleaded, "Will anyone help me with these orphans?" That night Harry and Bertha Holt wondered what they could do. "We are just a poor farm family," they said. But they prayed and kept thinking about it. Then Harry got an idea. An unreal, unbelievable, impossible idea for an Oregon farmer. Why not go to Korea and find some poor girl and bring her back to live on the farm? He decided to give it a try. He took the first step. But once in Korea, something happened to the initial idea and when Harry returned he presented Bertha with eight children. Bertha almost dropped dead from shock. "Honey, I couldn't help it," he said. "I think we have to adopt them."

Some of you know that adopting these children required an act of Congress. "Well," said Harry, "I guess that's what we will have to do." So he wrote his congressman, and pretty soon the United States Congress passed an act enabling Harry and Bertha to adopt these children.

A news photo of Harry and Bertha and their new family made the wire services, and in no time at all letters began pouring in asking how more people could help. A few months later Harry thought a little bigger, chartered an airplane, and filled it with orphans. And when that plane landed back in Oregon there were fathers and mothers from all over the United States waiting to adopt these kids.

Not long ago Mrs. Holt was saluted at a banquet at the Beverly Hilton Hotel for their achievement. On that festive occasion, Bertha said, "It's hard for me to believe that we have actually provided homes in the United States for over 16,000 children. And we have 3,000 that we are taking care of alone right now, many of them children of our soldiers in Vietnam."

I don't know what God wants you do, but I know this: *God does his greatest things through simple people who dare to begin.* It's the miracle of beginnings. When God drops his ideas into a believer's mind, watch out. Something fantastic is going to happen.

The truth is that every human being is a potential receptacle for God's voice. Every human brain is designed so that it can think and receive God's ideas and God's thoughts. God has a plan for your life. He will give you an idea. When a positive idea strikes your mind, all you have to do is start and wings will break out. Suddenly an ordinary life becomes extraordinary. A little person becomes a big person when he lets God's idea come alive in his life. And that's the secret to greatness. If you want to walk through the gateway to the great way, *start!*

The Law of Emotional Gravity

Getting started! How do you do it? To get started requires breaking the psychic inertia that keeps you at a standstill. Even as there is a physical law of gravity, so there is a law of emotional gravity. There is a powerful emotional inclination in every human life to play it safe, to take it easy. This produces a downward drag of incredible addictive power with infinite destructive consequences. It literally kills!

It's this law that keeps the overweight person from losing weight, because "I've never been able to stay on my diet." He's tried so often and failed that he passes by a new possibility. And, in the process, literally destroys his physical health. The person who won't exercise kills himself. He amusingly rejects, or brilliantly rationalizes his inaction, and as a result lets his youthful fitness decline until it breaks down like a building that has been left to the ravages of time. It's sad, because the physical body can be maintained. Life can be prolonged. Instead of gradual decline, with the last feeble years spent in stiff, senile sickness, the body and the brain can continue to function with brightness, keenness, and alertness into the advancing years. The secret, of course, is keeping physically fit. And this happens when you decide to begin, break loose from the normal, natural inclination to give in to emotional gravity.

Snapping the Trap

What does it take to break loose? To begin? To snap the trap that holds you back? Sometimes all it takes is a needle.

I met my needle when I was forty-five years old. Over the years I had gradually gained weight. Never in my life had I been athletic, nor had I done any form of exercise. That is, not until my needle appeared. His name? Walt Frederick, then general superintendent of maintenance in a Southern California school district. Like myself, he, too, had never been athletic. At the age of fifty-nine, he was fat—too fat to get out of the bathtub. But then a possibility-pregnant idea came into his mind. He began to wonder if by exercise he could bring the old body back into shape again—perhaps he could lose weight and become physically fit.

Walt began to diet. As the months passed, he started a program of walking, then running, until at the age of sixty-one he was slim, trim, and ran twenty-eight miles—in the Boston marathon!

As I write these pages, Walt is nearing seventy, but he remains youthful and continues to run several miles every day. He is in better physical condition than 80 percent of the college-age youth in America.

One day he came to me, "God has told me that I am to be your trainer," he said. "I want you to live a long life, and to be vitally alive as long as you live. But you must lose weight, start running, and get in shape." Amazingly, I began—and I succeeded! But not until the trap of emotional gravity was snapped.

Deep-seated habits continued to hold me down. I found

excuses for not exercising. I found that I was incapable of breaking my bad eating habits. I was in a trap until I got Walt's letter. That letter! I think I knew what it would say even before I opened it. The truth is, I didn't open it for months. I didn't dare to read it. So I kept it in my briefcase, until one day, on an airplane, I somehow got the courage to read it. Believe me, it hit me at the deepest level. It snapped the trap. This is what it said:

Dear Dr. Schuller:
I happen to be the trainer—*the needle.*

In passing your wife the other Sunday on the walk, I asked about your training. She was embarrassed to admit that you had become lax in your physical training—that you were too busy. To me, of course, that's a laugh and a cop-out. Next to our spiritual fitness, physical fitness comes. If we get so busy trying to help others that we neglect our own souls and bodies, we fall prey to (as Solomon says), "I was so busy keeping other's vineyards, my own I have not kept."

The following soliloquy came to me:

We can become spiritual backsliders.

We can also backslide physically.

We fend off spiritual backsliding by raising our consciousness by Bible readings and inspired writings.

We fend off physical deterioration by stimulating reading every day, such as *Runners World*, etc. Take it along on your trips.

We renew our soul by actual fellowship with spiritually minded people.

How long since you talked to a good athlete about physical fitness?

It's easy to lose interest in the Christian way if we are only spectator Christians and do not participate in Christian work.

Many people are but spectators of fitness for other athletic bodies but do not have the motivation to do anything for themselves but get soft and flabby until they like it that way.

Excuses keep most people from being practicing Christians. We know there are no reasons.

Excuses keep people from physical fitness. There are no overriding reasons to the thinking person for being slothful physically.

People backslide spiritually because they do not keep before them the importance of keeping their spirit in pursuit of spiritual excellence.

People become flabby physically because they do not emphatically and stirringly remind themselves that their body is the Temple of God. He can only partly come to fruition in a neglected body.

We can neglect spiritual exercise and become spiritually unhealthy and succumb to various spiritual diseases.

Neglect of these bodies that are only tuned up and kept in shape by exercise makes us weak and susceptible to psychosomatic diseases that the person in shape shakes off and resists in the subconscious workings of a healthy body.

The path of least resistance has led to many a good Christian's downfall.

The path of take it easy now has led to many a good star to physical downfall.

Procrastination in carrying out the practices of Christianity has led many to become weak. Vacillating and give-up-itis.

Procrastination physically leads to a lessening of the urge to live vigorously until one becomes but a shadow of former strength.

A Christian backslides spiritually when he becomes lazy about attaining goals in Christian living.

If we lose our goals of fitness, we deteriorate.

RESULTS OF BACKSLIDING

Spiritually	*Physically*
Loss of self-esteem	Same
Loss of esteem for others	Same
Loss of our leadership place	Same
Loss of stamina and endurance	Same
Become spiritually sluggish	Same
Become spiritually sick	Same
Give up spiritual for lesser things	Same
Eventually leads to spiritual death	Same
Leads to a hardened conscience as we drift	Same
Become spiritually useless	Same
Near the end regrets (If I only had ...)	Same
At last too late	Same

Could be rather doleful. But need not be so. Believe me, early in the morning, out under the stars, as I exercise, breathe deep and skip rope, I believe for you that you will, that morning, rise up and throw off all sluggishness of body as I know you do of the

spirit, and run and not be weary. Help the healthful genes along
that God gave you in your strong Iowa farm heritage.

God bless you. Be in health.

Walt Frederick

Principles for Getting Started

I want to be your needle. Here are two "needle principles"
to give you self-starting power.

1. IT'S LATER THAN YOU THINK

It's obvious from Walt's letter that this principle got me going. "Someday I'll do it," can quickly lead you past the point
of no return. Do it now, start today before it's too late. Like
Kierkegaard's goose who procrastinated until it was too fat
to fly, the inevitable end of "I'll do it tomorrow" is never getting started—and finally being unable to start.

You have the freedom to turn away from the alluring call
to ease and comfort that leaves you trapped in the grip of
emotional gravity. You can tear yourself loose. Be strong! Be
a starter while you can. It's not too late until you give up and
surrender to defeat. What you decide to do now will determine the rest of your life. Neglect to start now, and you will
soon develop an undisciplined habit that will never let you go.

Until you learn how to start, all of the rest of your knowledge,
training, talent, and experience will be of little lasting value.

2. USE YOUR HEAD AND YOUR HEART WILL FOLLOW

I have used this principle successfully in three specific ways.
You already know how Walt Frederick was my needle in get-

ting me to lose weight and to exercise. But I could only succeed when I put my head before my heart. The same principle applied to quitting smoking. I began smoking cigarettes
in college and I was soon hooked. Having been raised in a
religious environment where smoking was not considered sin-
ful, I was under no pressure to quit. That is, not until I found
out smoking causes cancer, which could kill me. It has been
years now since I have smoked.

I would not have lost weight, started exercising, or stopped
smoking until I made up my mind and let my heart follow.
If you wait until you feel like it you will never begin. Right
now, as I write these lines, I am in Honolulu. Three morn-
ings ago I was in Lucerne, Switzerland. While I was there I
ran four miles before breakfast. On my way here I stopped
in Washington, D.C. where I did my running at Dulles airport. Yesterday and this morning I have been running here
in Honolulu.

Only I didn't feel like it this morning. Yesterday I gave a
lecture and I'm still experiencing jet lag. You will understand,
then, why I felt like skipping it this morning. But I know the
secret. If I do what my head tells me is the right thing, I will
soon begin to "feel" like it after a while. Sure enough! After
I ran two miles this morning I was getting the spirit. Now I
feel absolutely fantastic. So here is the secret. *Develop the self-
discipline to produce life-changing willpower by deliberately choosing
and planning to get yourself hooked on good habits.* Think about
the best health, happiness, and spiritual power-producing
habits you can have, and then develop a plan to get yourself
addicted to these personal habits. Always remember to use
your head and your heart will follow. Start with your heart
and you will fail. Lead with your head and you will win.

Today, and every day of my life, I feed my habits. I nourish my positive addictions, and I know that if I ever give up I am finished. Once hooked, it's easier to keep my positive habit going—to remain a free, liberated person than to return to the enjoyment of tobacco, fattening foods, and the slovenly life-style that slowly but surely leads to the decay of spirit and body. So I truly enjoy the clean taste in my mouth from not smoking. I enjoy the table without eating fattening foods; and I also enjoy the youthful running feeling more than the tired old lazy feeling.

If you want to get started, program your mind like the computer it is, and it will feed back to the body and to your heart what you have programmed into the brain. You must do this because your subconscious has no scruples. Your computer-like brain will play back whatever you order it to do. You can feed into your mind the positive, personal behavior modification instructions, and then you can be certain that with sincere follow-up cooperation on your part, your heart will surely, absolutely get the message. You are on your way. You have started. You will be a Supersuccess with self-esteem and pride.

Keep on using these principles for the rest of your life. For as long as we live we will have to deal with the everpresent tension of "emotional gravity"—that mysterious force and inclination to take the easy road. So let your head be the needle to prick your heart. Once you know what to do, start doing it, and soon you will want to do it. Beginning is Succeeding.

8 Count the Apples in a Seed

Any time you have a positive thought, an impulse, an idea, a suggestion, an opportunity, or a dream, look upon them as possible angels from Heaven, gifts from God. Grab hold of them. Don't let the great opportunity escape. Do something now! Act, ask, telephone someone, write a letter, make a note of it. Write it on your calendar. Schedule an appointment. Do something! Don't let the flighty butterfly escape. Cage it. If you can't handle it right now, at least take an option on it so that it doesn't get away from you.

Every time you respond positively to a Possibility Thought you are planting a seed. Here is a principle that goes to the heart of Possibility Thinking philosophy: *Any fool can count the seeds in an apple, but only God can count the apples in a seed.*

I have discovered that Supersuccessful People take every good idea they run into and act upon it. Not all will bear fruit but some will. Throw enough good seeds on the ground and surely some of them will sprout. Do this and you will have enough projects going so that you will never fear waking up some morning with nothing to do. With all these exciting possibilities before you, you need simply to organize your time in such a way that you are handling the most important projects that command priority on your time and attention today.

The Apple-Seed System

Count the apples in a seed! Let this idea saturate your thinking and you will be lead to unlimited prosperity. All success starts with an idea that comes from God. And a God-inspired idea is a seed that has immeasurable, almost infinite growth potential.

In 1954 I was living in Chicago, Illinois, and I was twenty-eight years old. I had $500. I was given the opportunity to come to California and start a new church, from scratch. At the time I had no idea what the results of this design would be. I could have rejected it, but if I had done so my ministry would be far less than it is today. By prayerfully responding to this possibility impregnated idea—this special seed that came as a gift from God—I now minister to millions of people every week by television in America, Canada, and Australia. It happened because I saw the original idea as a seed from God to be planted.

Two dynamic young men from Grand Rapids, Michigan, Jay Van Andel and Richard De Vos, got an idea several years ago for a marketing plan to sell their products. They saw the idea as a seed loaded with growth potential and self-multiplication powers. They grabbed hold and today there are tens of thousands of private businessmen and women around the world selling Amway Products. Several of the salespersons are millionaires. But note this: Because I know many of them personally, I can affirm that they acquire great wealth in order to share it to help other people, causes, and institutions. In that way they are fulfilling what we are defining as success in this book: *Building self-esteem for yourself and others through honest service.*

Mary Kay Ash's story is another illustration of the apples-in-a-seed system at work. With a handful of dollars and ideas, she started. After a month in her new business, her husband died. But her sons, Richard and Ben, helped her and she kept going. Soon she developed a line of good skin-care products and built a marketing system based on the principle of unselfish sharing of the profits with her national consultants and directors.

At a recent convention attended by the 10,000 independent salespersons in Mary Kay's organization, I was asked to give an address. I was tremendously impressed when I found that a sharecropper's daughter from a tiny town in Georgia, a Mexican-American from a border state, a young black from a Chicago ghetto, and a seventy-two-year-old white woman from a village in Texas ran off with the national awards. Many of these private businesswomen are earning well over $50,000 a year—some even $100,000. All because Mary Kay Ash had an idea—an "apple-seed idea." *Business Week* magazine has listed her as one of the one-hundred top American businesswomen.

The apple-seed system really works. In fact, it works so well that I need to offer a word of caution. It can produce negative results, too. Years ago two men emigrated from Scotland to Northern California. Each brought something that was meaningful to them from their homeland. One brought the seeds of the national symbol of Scotland, the thistle. The other brought honeybees. To this day, farmers battle the thistle. And to this very day, also, there are honeybees making honey in the mountains and in the forests. You can decide if you are going to plant thistles or breed honeybees. You can decide what you are going to do with your life. You can plant it and make an investment for good and for God, or you can waste it. So know this: *Beginnings make a difference, and you can control your beginnings!*

The first time I visited my late friend, Chun Young Chang, in Korea, we walked past a fruitmarket in Taegu. I saw the largest and most beautiful red apples I have seen anywhere. I said to my friend, Chun, "I didn't know they raised apples in Korea." He replied, "Well, they didn't until about seventy-five years ago when a Scottish Presbyterian missionary came to Korea, bringing apple seeds with him. He planted the seeds and when the first apples appeared, he spread the seeds throughout the countryside. Today it is the number one fruit product in this country."

Who can count the apples in a seed?

Who can count the power in one dedicated life? Just a little baby born in a manger.

Not very important. Just a child from a poor peasant mother and a simple father! Today, two thousand years later, untold millions of people around the world draw inspiration from Jesus Christ.

Dr. Henry Poppen, who spent over forty years as a missionary to China, once shared with me his experience of going to a remote village, where presumably missionaries had never been. There he told the people about Jesus, how he was gentle and kind, and that he was able to forgive easily and loved even those who were unlovable.

When Dr. Poppen finished telling them about Jesus, some of the men came to him and said, "We know Jesus! He has been here."

"No," said Dr. Poppen. "He lived and died in a country that is far away from here."

"No, no," they replied. "He died here. Come. We'll show you his grave."

They led him outside the city to a cemetery where only one American was buried. There on the tombstone was the name of a Christian medical doctor, who, all on his own, felt called by Jesus Christ to go there, live there, and die there. Now the people thought he was Jesus, the very person Dr. Poppen told them about.

Who can measure the influence of one dedicated solitary life? Who can count the apples in a seed?

Another incident in Dr. Poppen's life occurred after nearly forty years in China. The communist regime called him to a public trial. Over ten thousand people jammed the square as they listened to one trumped up charge after another read against him. Finally, he was declared guilty and ordered to leave the country. He and his wife and two other missionaries boarded a bus and went to Swatow, hoping to catch a steamer to Hong Kong on their way to America. But in Swatow Dr. Poppen was pulled off the bus and imprisoned in a 4'×6' cell. He didn't know what was to happen to him, but he did know that most missionaries who were prisoners of Mao Tse-tung never lived to tell about it. While his wife made her way to Hong Kong, Dr. Poppen stayed in his cell, trying to keep his sanity by singing the hymns he loved. But after four and a half days he could stand the blackness and the mental torture no longer. At midnight he got on his knees and prayed by his small wooden cot, "Oh, God, you know I am not St. Paul, or the Apostle John or Peter, I am only Henry Poppen, and Henry Poppen can take no more. Lord, deliver me or take my life."

He fell asleep on his hands and knees, only to be awakened about an hour later. The guards came in, tied a rope around his neck with a slipknot, ran it down his backbone, and bound his arms behind him so tightly that if he struggled he would strangle himself. Then he was led down a dark, winding cobblestone street until he saw a reflection of light in rippling water. He heard the hum and chunking of an engine, and he saw the dark outline of an ocean steamer, waiting with its gangplank down. The guards shoved him on deck and said, "Now, get out of our country."

The gangplank was raised, and the steamer blew its whistle. The captain took the rope off his neck and cut it loose from his hands. Dr. Poppen raised his head in gratitude, a free man under God! But he had left forty years behind him, and when he returned to America he was, for a time, discouraged and defeated. That the Communists had wiped out the labor of a lifetime was a negative, discouraging thought. But he underestimated the power of the seed.

Not long ago I visited Hong Kong with my missionary friend, David Wong. David had just come back from a thirty-five-day tour through the interior of China with exciting news. "There are more Christians in China today than ever before," he said, "they meet secretly and privately, but they are there!"

Seeds planted years ago are still reproducing. Count the apples in a seed. Only God knows how many there are!

One of my favorite people is Christy Wilson—a living legend in Afghanistan. Working as a missionary-educator in that poverty-oppressed country, Christy shared the tragedy of the near wipe-out of the nation's leading industry—sheep breeding. A fatal disease had entered the flocks and stubbornly resisted efforts to eradicate it. With the entire sheep industry in danger of extinction, it meant that there was a loss of wool for clothing, leather for commercial products, and food to eat. In a country already suffering mass poverty, the potential losses were catastrophic.

Christy Wilson understands prayer better than most people. "What can I do?" he prayed. The answer came: "Write to your friends in the United States and ask them to send you some Long Island ducks." So this is what Christy did. Not long afterwards two dozen duck eggs were shipped air freight from New York. But they didn't reach Afghanistan directly! The shipment was side-tracked and spent too many hot days in a warehouse in Calcutta. When the package finally arrived in Kabul, Afghanistan, some of the eggs were cracked and smelled rotten. Christy prayed again, "Lord, let at least two eggs hatch out, and let one of them be male and the other female."

Twenty-two eggs proved to be rotten and infertile. Only two hatched—one was male and the other female. In a matter of months they were reproducing, and the offspring multiplied.

Then the miracle happened! The ducks began to devour the snails that crawled along the watering holes where the sheep went to drink. Amazingly, the fatal sheep disease disappeared! For the snails proved to be the carriers of the disease. Today both ducks and the sheep are in abundance. For which Christy Wilson was signally honored by the king himself.

Every Good Deed Is a Fertile Seed

The apple-seed system works in other ways too. It applies to a word of encouragement rightly spoken and to a noble act of love sincerely extended.

I read once about a woman, a person who has remained anonymous, who went to an orphanage in Iowa and asked, "Is there an orphan here that nobody wants?" The matron of the orphanage said, "Indeed, there is. She's ten years old, ugly to look at and has a terrible hunchback. She is sickly, ill-tempered, cross and irritable. The only thing beautiful about her is her name, Mercy Goodfaith. We have long since given up hope of getting her adopted." The nameless woman said, "That's exactly the child I want—Mercy Goodfaith!"

Thirty-five years later, when the head of the Orphanage Inspection Department was checking out orphanages, he turned in a report about this one particular orphanage, which said, "This orphanage is outstanding. It is exquisitely clean. The food is wonderful. And all this is attributed to the matron of the place, out of whose soul there oozes love.

"When I dropped in for an unexpected inspection, it was dinnertime. At the close of the dinner, the matron said, 'Girls and boys, let's do what we always do after dinner,' and with that they all moved into the living room. One of the girls sat at the piano and all the children started singing Christmas songs. The matron herself sat in a big, overstuffed chair with huge armrests that were about a foot wide. Two little girls sat on one arm of the chair, two boys on the other, and two other children sat on her lap. Two other boys leaned behind the big chair, hands spread and palms against the big back. From time to time they would stroke the matron's hair. One little girl was curled at her feet and played with the silky dress against his upper lip. Never did I see such beautiful eyes as those in that matron. So beautiful that I almost forgot how ugly her face was and how huge and gruesome was her hunchback. Her name was Mercy Goodfaith!"

Because Mercy Goodfaith was the object of a nameless love, she multiplied that love manifold. How many apples were in that seed? Only God knows.

All of the Flowers of All of the Tomorrows Are in the Seeds of Today. That's the reason I am an optimist. The only excuse for being a pessimist would be if we could wipe out of the human family all the seed-acts of goodness, truth, and love.

Let me tell you now how one of those seeds came to me. I have made, in recent years, two trips to Russia. On one of them, I made contact with a new Christian, and I asked him, "How did you become a believer when you were indoctrinated from childhood in atheism?"

He pointed to the great cathedral in Red Square—a fantastic work of architectural art, built hundreds of years ago. "That building was the key," he said, "I marvelled at it and wondered who built it. What were they like? What books did they read? Where did they draw their inspiration?"

The question provoked inquiry, and the young atheist was led down a road that brought him to a book, the Bible. He read it, and that led to his faith in God. The builders of that cathedral never imagined that one day their country would fall under an atheistic regime, and that their cathedral would remain a silver silhouette, silently speaking its strong sermons to future generations.

Nor did the builders dream that their work would serve as an inspiration to a pastor, centuries later, in a country called America, in a state called California. I returned from Russia to find that we needed to build a larger building to handle the crowds coming to our church in Garden Grove. The church board calculated that we would need a 4,100-seat cathedral.

With that in mind, I engaged Philip Johnson, one of the purest architects in the world today. "Design a cathedral that will last for centuries and inspire future generations to ask questions: 'Who built it? What did they believe? What books did they read?'"

The famed architect took the challenge, but then asked, "What dollar budget must I work with?" "You need not consider dollars," I told him. "You should only consider designing a structure that, by its beauty, function, drama, and art form will be a joy forever. I have borrowed $200,000 to get you started.

"If possible," I further advised him, "make it an all glass-crystal cathedral—an all-aglow structure without a gloomy corner to hide any of God's beautiful sky." Three months later the model was finished. It made national news overnight, "Crystal Cathedral Designed for California Church," the headlines said.

Now we were faced with the question of costs—over $10,000,000. And we were still burdened with a mortgage on our present property. But then an idea emerged. What if we got several people to give one million each? An impossible idea! As I write this chapter, several people have already committed one million dollars each. The project will be completed. The crystal cathedral will be built debt-free, not long after this book is published. Now here is an amazing thing. All of the million-dollar donors were once poor people. All were common people who discovered an idea—and acted on it—planted the seed—prospered—and part of the fruit of their planted seed will stand in the form of a great glass cathedral that will become the center of our ministry to millions around the world through television.

Who can count the apples in a seed!

Plant the Seed Ideas Now

On the Iowa farm where I grew up, I remember that for many years my dad needed all the grain from the previous year's crop to feed the livestock. But there was always one corner of the grain bin where he stored the corn that was to be used as seed for next spring's planting. Sometimes he was so desperately short of food for his cattle that I am sure he was tempted to use the seed he had stored away, but he never did. He could have used it, and on the short run it would have produced milk for his children. But he had another option. He could put the seed in the ground at planting time to produce still more corn. But this option meant taking a risk. There were at least seven things that could happen to his seed corn.

First, some of it might prove to be infertile, in which case it would rot. Second, there might not be enough rain, which meant that the seed would not sprout. Third, some of the seed might sprout, but would then be choked to death by weeds. Fourth, some of it might sprout, grow big, and then be eaten by insects. Fifth, some of the seed might grow into healthy plants, then be cut down by hail or wind, or else destroyed by a tornado. Sixth, some of it might shoot itself up, but then just before the new ears start to set, the weather could change and all that would be left is the stalk and a cob with no kernels.

All that could happen. But here was a seventh possibility. It might sprout, grow, survive the insects, storms, the changes in the weather—and it might grow to full fruition and produce a beautiful new ear of corn. That one kernel could multiply more than a hundredfold.

If my dad had given thought to those six dire possibilities, his dream would have died right there. Instead, he thought only of one possibility—that the seed would become productive. So he planted the seed before he had any guarantees that the disastrous problems could be overcome.

Success Requires Absolute Faith

God drops his seed thoughts. The problem is that most of us are not willing to pay the price to succeed. That price is faith—absolute faith. In order to turn an apple seed into an apple tree, there must be unquestioned faith in the seed. It takes a lot of faith to take a seed and bury it in the ground and to keep on believing in the power of that seed.

Do you know about the olive trees in California? They originally came from the Mediterranean region. One Sunday I excitedly offered to send my TV viewers live little olive trees. In no time at all we were mailing out tens of thousands of them, and never did I get more negative mail. But one letter from New York was different. Here it is:

My dear Dr. Schuller: I have received the olive tree and wish to thank you. Permit me to take a moment of your precious time to tell you about my experience. What a thrill I had when the postman delivered the little box. I was so excited and happy. I gently opened the carton and to my surprise found a plastic bag with a tiny plastic box and dried-out twig. What a letdown! I could have cried. I felt as though this little innocent olive tree had smothered and withered inside this plastic bag on the long trip from California to New York.

Well for some reason I didn't throw it away. I transplanted that olive twig. While doing so I felt sorry for it because it had dried out and withered and the leaves were folded down and most had fallen off. I soaked this poor twig thoroughly and gave it a good drink. I placed it on a table facing the East sun. I felt so foolish keeping this dead twig and giving it so much attention. But after several days, a surprise! The leaves had lifted and the tiny branch had turned itself to the sun.

I am so delighted now, words can't express my gratitude to you. I just love it. And I will keep you informed as to its growth.

Now I wonder how many olive trees were thrown away as dead twigs because people didn't have the faith to believe there was still life in those roots, even though we sent instructions along with the mailings. And I wonder, too, how many people have lost faith, too soon, in their dreams.

Who can count the olives in a twig that looks so bare! Who can count the apples in a seed!

Is God giving you a dream? Is he trying to tell you what you should be doing with your life? I want to tell you one thing: If God gives you a dream, it will scare you because it will be big and impossible. But have faith. Stay with the dream. With God's help, it will work out great.

Where do you start? Chances are, your greatest opportunities are in your own backyard.

9 Bloom Where You Are Planted

Plant your seeds where you are, and you will bloom where you are planted.

Did you know that you are sitting on a gold mine? Many people don't know it; some people won't believe it; others suspect it but don't dare to take the action that will lead to the profit-making that is available to them. Almost everyone is surrounded by opportunities that are as rich as any gold mine.

One of the poorest countries on earth is the Central African Republic. Two million impoverished people live there. In 1964 the United States sent a satellite into orbit to measure the electromagnetic field around the earth. About four years ago some geophysicists decided to run an experiment on the side, using the satellite. They wondered if there was a jet stream in the ionosphere over the equator, so they directed the satellite to cross the equator over the Central African Republic. What they found is that every time the satellite passed over this coun-

111

try, the monitoring needles went wild. Finally they determined the cause of this hyperactivity. They calculated that there is an area 125 miles wide, 450 miles long, and 20 miles deep that holds the largest untapped iron mine in the world, dwarfing the Mesabi Range in Minnesota. If this scientific prediction proves true, then that country of two million people will tap the tremendous wealth that God has put beneath their feet.

Bloom where you are planted. Prosperity is within your grasp.

In writing to the church in Philippi, St. Paul added a thought at the end of his letter: "All the saints greet you, chiefly they that are of Caesar's household" (Phil. 4:22). St. Paul was writing from Rome where he was held prisoner. And there he had discovered the most amazing thing. Even with all its viciousness, immoralities, and crimes, there were Christians in Caesar's palace. It's like saying that committed Christians have infiltrated the core of communist cells in Eastern Europe. God has a way of scattering seeds everywhere. They bloom in the most unlikely places.

Bloom where you are. Your attitude, more than anything else, will determine whether you are a success or a failure.

J. W. Moran tells of visiting a friend and discovering some beautiful flowers pressed in his friend's old Bible. He neither knew the name nor the description of them, so he asked his friend about them.

"These flowers are Scottish poppies," his friend said. "We discovered them on an expedition up a lonely promontory on the coast of New Zealand. My wife and I were exploring the region when we came across this profusion of blooming flowers. What they were and where they came from we did not know. We were mystified to see them blooming in such an unlikely place. Evidently a seed blew in from a passing steamer and it found its way into that little crevice because the flowers are found in no other place in New Zealand."

Flowers in a rocky promontory! Saints in Caesar's household! Bloom where you are planted. Chances are, right under your feet, wherever you are, there is a beautiful opportunity waiting for you—now!

While visiting New Zealand recently, I was told that one hundred miles north of Auckland are the caves of Waitomo—among the eight great wonders of the world. Once a farmer owned the area, then sold it, not knowing the treasure he had under his land. Here, when you make your way down into the caves, you come to an underground river where you board a little boat and are told by a guide "not to utter a sound."

The guide silently glides the boat through the inky darkness by placing his hands along the wet walls of the damp underground canyon. The blackness is total. Then suddenly you spot the little sparkling lights. For a moment you think you are in a desert on a clear night, seeing the Milky Way far above you. Actually, the lights are only four feet above your head. What you see are the glowing lights of millions of glowworms that live in the caves. Twinkling and glowing like a galaxy of little neon lights. You can, if you are very still, hear the chorus of the buzzing of these beautiful creatures, who sound like a heavenly choral concert.

Once God said to Moses, "What is in your hand?" Moses answered, "A rod." God must have smiled and said, "Ah, but don't underestimate that rod."

What's under your feet? What's in your hand? Here are

four simple and workable tips that will help you bloom where you are planted. You can be a flower in a craggy wall, a saint in Caesar's palace. You can be a positive thinker in a world of negative thinkers. You can bloom where you are.

1. Believe that God has no Wastebaskets

To bloom where you are planted may test your positive thinking to the limit, but remember this principle: There's a purpose for every place and every person under the sun. God doesn't believe in waste. There is nothing that, in his mind, has to be thrown away as worthless.

I recently read a story in a hotel room in Tokyo: "There was a Chinese wife who said to her husband, 'I would like a new coat.' Her husband said to her, 'What will you do with your old coat?' She said, 'I will make a bed cover out of it.' He said, 'What will you do with your old bed cover?' She replied, 'I will make pillowcases out of it.' He said, 'What will you do with the old pillowcases?' She said, 'I will make new cleaning cloths.' He said, 'What will you do with the old cleaning cloths?' She said, 'I will tie them together and make a mop out of them.' He said, 'What will you do with the old mop?' She said, 'I will chop it up in little pieces, mix it with cement, and we will patch the holes in our cottage in the springtime.' He said, 'All right. You may have a new coat.'"

If a person can find a good purpose and use to everything—what can God do? God has no wastebaskets. He has a purpose for every place and every person under the sun. Think positively and start to bloom where you are.

2. BELIEVE THE BEST ABOUT EVERY SITUATION

Look for the best in every place, and believe the best about every person. That's an essential attitude of all Supersuccessful Possibility Thinking persons.

Consider the experience of a businessman on the Long Island commuter train, going into New York City. An unshaven man in a shabby coat brushed close to him, jostling him in the crush of the passengers. As the unshaven man moved toward the exit, the Long Island businessman felt his pocket and discovered his wallet was missing. Just then the train stopped and the door opened. The businessman grabbed the shoulder of the fellow who bumped him. Thus captured, the grubby culprit turned around with a horrified, frightened look on his face, desperately lunged forward, breaking free from his coat, and jumped off the train, just as the doors were again closing. Inside the train, the businessman stood holding the villain's coat. Immediately he went through the pockets, expecting to find his wallet. Alas! they were empty. So, frustrated in his triumph, he proceeded to his office where he found a phone call waiting for him. It was his wife who had called to say that he had left his wallet at home on the dresser that morning.

That's how wars and divorces start, and that's how problems in corporations begin—believing the worst about other people. Someone jumps to a negative conclusion, and the spiral begins to turn downward. The most dangerous person in the world is a negative thinker who puts two and two together. Believe the best about others. Think positively. Believe the best about persons, positions and institutions.

3. BE A POSITIVE REACTIONARY

It's not what happens to you but how you react to circumstances that determines whether you will bloom where you
are, or dry up where you are. So develop the habit of reacting positively to negative conditions.

There was a man who was stricken with an illness that
left him totally paralyzed. A friend who hadn't seen him for
many years came to his bedside and was struck by the change
in his countenance and personality that had followed this
lengthy illness. Looking at his beautiful face as he was resting
in bed, the friend said, "Sickness and trouble really colors
a personality, doesn't it?" The paralyzed man replied, "Yes,
it does, and I decided that I would choose the colors and make
them beautiful."

If you choose to react positively to a negative condition
you turn the situation around by converting a negative into
a positive. That's exciting.

Then develop the habit of *reacting positively to positive conditions*. React positively to negative conditions; react positively
to positive conditions. A fear of failure could tempt you to
react negatively. So what you must do is dissolve the natural
fear of failure by saying, "I've got an idea. I think it may be
a God-given idea. I don't know if it will be a successful or
a nonsuccessful idea, so I will become a researcher and an
experimenter. I will try it. If it works, great! If it doesn't prove
to be successful, I will have been a successful researcher. I
will have found it doesn't work."

With this attitude you will be successful every time, for
researchers never fail. Every scientist knows this. A failed
effort is a demonstration of what won't work. But that's not

failure. It is only a sign that there are other methods and procedures waiting to be discovered that will work. So think positively, try positively, and tackle your problems creatively.

4. TRUST GOD CONFIDENTLY

You didn't ask to be born. You had nothing to do with your parentage, the color of your skin, your national origin, your station in life, and probably not even with where you are living. But God has been guiding you. He has a plan for you. St. Paul writes: "And I am sure that he who began a good work in you will bring it to completion at the day of Jesus Christ" (Phil. 1:6, RSV).

Dare to believe that. Trust God confidently. You can be the saint in Caesar's household. You can bloom where you are planted. God will use you if you trust him. *So throw away your wastebasket and replace it with a tackle box.* Tackle your problems positively, creatively, and prayerfully.

Truly, God wants every flower to bloom. He wants every seed to sprout. He wants every person to be happy. On the night before Jesus died, Jesus prayed, "Father, I pray that my joy might be in them, and that their joy might be complete" (John 15:11). That is a remarkable thing. In the face of his own cruel death, Jesus prayed for your happiness, your joy.

Diamonds Are Where You Are

Undoubtedly, the most beautiful crown ever fashioned is the one designed for the Princess of Iran. The incredibly beautiful diamonds that are part of that crown defy description and are, quite literally, the international banking collateral for that country.

Many of the diamonds in that crown come from the famous Golconda mine. It is the same mine where the Kohinoor diamond in the crown jewels of England comes from, and where the Orloff diamond in the crown jewels of Russia was found. Golconda is also the source of the well-known story told years ago by Russell Conwell called, "Acres of Diamonds."

According to Conwell, there was once a man named Ali Hafed, who lived in Persia. He was a farmer. He had a wife, children, some sheep, camels, and he raised wheat on his land. He was a contented and happy man and, according to his standards, also rich.

His contentment with his lot in life ended one day, however, when a priest told him about a strange stone that sparkled like a million suns. Ali Hafed had never heard of diamonds, but now that he had learned about these beautiful gems, he was determined to have some for himself. "Where can I find diamonds?" he asked the priest. "Look for a stream that flows through white sands surrounded by high mountains," the priest told him.

So Ali Hafed sold his farm, left his wife and children, and set out on a journey to find diamonds. He traveled for many years, searching for a stream that flowed through white sands, surrounded by high mountains. With the passing years, he one day found himself broke and destitute, on the lonely coast of Spain. Utterly defeated, he plunged into the sea and died.

Meanwhile, the man who bought Ali Hafed's farm found one day an odd black rock while watering his camel. He took it home and thought no more about it, until a priest came to visit him. The priest examined the black rock and suddenly saw a flash of color from a crack in it. "A diamond! Where did you get it?" the priest asked. "By the cool sands and white stream near the high mountains where I water my camel," the man said.

Together, they ran to the stream, where they scratched and dug with their hands. They found more diamonds. Their discovery is now known as Golconda mine, the greatest diamond mine in the world.

Diamonds were in Ali Hafed's backyard, yet he spent a lifetime in a fruitless search. And so, often, do we. We can spend our lives in all kinds of travels and pursuits of pleasure, fame, and wealth, when all the time what we are looking for can be found right beneath our own feet.

Bloom where you are planted. Wherever you are, God is. Wherever God is, there are beautiful plans, if only you can see the possibilities. God put you where you are because he sees diamonds in the rocks all around you.

Think of the great people of the world around whom history has turned. Where did they come from? London, Rome, Tokyo, New York City, Washington, Hong Kong? Some of them, surely. But the greatest did not live in those cities. Cyrus the Great came from Persepolis and his headquarters was there. Jesus of Nazareth came from Bethlehem. Gandhi from the streets of India. What does this prove? That success and greatness do not depend on the place where you come from or where you are. They depend on the person. The place does not make the person. The person makes the place.

That's exciting! Power, success, and achievement will come

to you anywhere you are if your attitude is right. That's why the people whose lives blossomed and literally changed the course of history, have often been headquartered in obscure places— places that later became famous because they were there.

How do you bloom where you are planted? By thinking of the possibilities, that's how. Look at the possibilities under your feet right now, whatever your situation. There are acres of diamonds under your feet now, diamonds of joy, happiness, and purposefulness in your life. All you need is a positive, dynamic attitude.

During World War II, a young man in training at an army base in one of the bleakest and most remote parts of the California desert took his new wife to live with him there, so they could be together before he went overseas. The only housing they could find was an old shack that had been abandoned by Indians. For a few days the young woman found life in this bleak place tolerable, but then the newness wore off and she became miserable. The winds came up and the sandstorms struck. The temperature went up to 115 degrees. Soon the loneliness overwhelmed her, and when her husband was assigned to two weeks training deeper in the desert, she reached the end of her rope. She wrote her mother that she couldn't take it and was coming home. Her mother answered immediately. The letter contained only three lines:

Dear Daughter,
Two men sit in prison bars.
One sees mud, the other stars.

The young woman read them over and over, until she thought, "I wonder what the stars look like from here." She went out of her shack and discovered what everyone in California knows. In no place in the world do the stars shine brighter than over the deserts of California. She thrilled to the beauty of the twinkling sky.

Inspired, she set out the next day to discover her community. She walked down the road to visit the Indians who lived in the shacks not far from her. She was sure they were unfriendly, because she had never talked with them. But then she began talking with two women who were weaving, and when they saw that she was sincere and friendly, they became friendly. When she stopped thinking they were hostile, they stopped being hostile. In a short time, she, too, was learning the art of basketweaving.

Then one day some Indian boys brought her seashells found in the desert, and told her the legend of how once the desert was an ocean. So she began to collect seashells in the desert and was fascinated by them. By the time her husband finished his tour of duty in that location, she had become an authority on the desert and had written a book about it. She fell in love with the desert, and she wept when it came time to say good-bye to her Indian friends.

Bloom where you are planted. I have learned that in whatever circumstance, condition, or place, with the help of God I can turn it into a garden. It's possible. If you keep that happy, positive attitude. It only requires faith that God didn't make a mistake when he brought you where you are. Wherever you are today, there are great possibilities. There are diamonds under your feet. Your life can bloom, if you will think positively and try to help someone around you. Get interested in someone else who is hurting.

Once a ship sailed from the Orient, along the coast of South America, where it had never sailed before. The crew misjudged its water requirements, and as it sailed along the Brazilian coast the supply became depleted. Seeing a passing ship with a South American flag, the captain sent out a distress signal, "Can you spare any water?" The message signaled back said, "Dip where you are!" So the captain dipped a bucket into the ocean, and found to his amazement that the ocean water was sweet. What he did not know was that the ship was in the center of a mile-wide current in the ocean where the Amazon River was still making its surging inrush into the ocean.

Learn that, wherever you find yourself, there are diamonds waiting to be mined, there is water to drink.

Attitude Counts More Than Latitude

Whether you are happy in life depends on what you are, not where you are. That's a fact. Some people who live in the desert are blossoming like a rose with joy and loving every minute of it. Others who live in the plush neighborhoods of modern American suburbs are miserable. Happiness depends on what you are, not where you are.

There's a story of a woman who spent her life looking for new places to live. Wherever she was, she was unhappy. The people were unfriendly. The climate was wrong. There was always someplace better, more attractive. This woman had a maid who had followed her for years, from residence to residence, from city to city. One day she said to her employer, "You can move as often as you want to, but nothing is going to change until you change you." It is that humble and simple truth which is at the core of this chapter. Happiness depends on you, not the property on which you live. Bloom where you are planted. And the desert will bloom like a rose. What you want in life is under your feet. It's closer to you than you can imagine if you have a positive attitude. No matter the circumstances, attitude is more important than latitude.

"That's easy for you to say," I can hear of you saying, "but what if you live in one of our inner city ghettos where there is poverty, blight and disease all around you. How could you possibly be happy there?" I'll tell you how. I don't think there is an inner city ghetto in any part of America that is more blighted than 146th Street, in South Bronx, New York City. I was there awhile ago, just before they dedicated a new $750,000 multi-purpose Christian Youth Center. Across the street is a heroin-shooting gallery. I walked up to the rooftops of the surrounding apartment buildings where I saw handfuls of fresh empty heroin sacks and a can wet at the bottom with drops of blood from the last junkie who had just given himself a fix.

There, right across the street, is the Mott Haven Reformed Church, and it's a rose in the desert. The members of that church are the most enthusiastic people in the world. And if you are enthusiastic, you are happy.

Asa Skinner and his wife, Nina, were members of my first church in Ivanhoe, a suburb of Chicago. One day Asa began having fainting spells and headaches, and an examination showed that he had a blood clot on the brain. After surgery, Asa was told that he would likely never go back to work again. He was confined to his home in a wheelchair when I came to visit him.

When I called on him a few weeks after he returned home from the hospital, I found him in his wheelchair out in the backyard, with high-powered binoculars in his hands. Next to him was a little table with pens and paper on it.

"How are you, Asa?" I inquired. "Oh, I'm marvelous," he said. "You know, there's a fantastic world out here." Then he began telling me about a bird building a nest and how he had been watching the eggs hatch out of their shells, about ants building a colony near his rosebush, and about the bees he had spotted nearby. His whole world had become that little world, and he found it throbbing with life and interest. He saw birth, death, struggle and challenge, and out of it all he gained strength. Three years later he was back to work.

And the desert shall bloom like a rose. Of course, it takes faith, trust, and belief. I truly believe that God has a beautiful and wonderful plan for your life. He'll never allow you to stay where you are unless there are diamonds under your feet.

Wherever you are, you are the center of something. In New York City, the people there say they are at the center of the world, and they are right. The people in Chicago say they are at the center of the United States and that the country revolves around them. They are also correct. Meanwhile, the people in Kansas City say they are at the hub of the nation. There's even a town in Idaho, where people are convinced that they are at the hub of the great Northwest. And if you look at a map, you will find that it's true. What is illustrated here is a great principle with far-reaching implications. *No matter where you are, you are in the center of the world,* and you can be great in your world.

One of the happiest people I know is David Lamb, a Chinese who lives in Calcutta, India. Calcutta is probably the most miserable city in the world. Of the four million people who live there, one million live, sleep, eat, excrete, breed, give birth and die on the sidewalks. It is a tragic scene. But Calcutta also has a slum section where you will find pigs sleeping on the sidewalks with the people.

When this positive-thinking Christian minister, David Lamb, discovered the slum section in Calcutta, he decided to go there and be a rose in that particular desert. He and his wife didn't have a dollar to their names, but they did have enthusiasm and they saw possibilities. Now he has three churches there, and every one is filled to overflowing with people whose average age is twenty-two years. With clean faces, sparkling eyes, hearts bubbling and rejoicing in the Lord, they sing, "Joyful, joyful, we adore thee, God of glory, God of love." And only two blocks away are pigs sleeping with people.

Jesus Christ really makes the difference. He can take a heart that is a desert and make it blossom like a rose. Believe that! Try it, and you will start rejoicing wherever you are.

With Possibility Thinking, you can be a Supersuccess; blooming where you are planted, regardless of your condition, your circumstances or your competition.

10 Use Competition Creatively

How do you react to competition? One thing all Supersuccessful People must learn is how to handle competition creatively. A person's life – his highs and lows, his successes and failures, his ambition and lethargy – can be analyzed in terms of how he handles competition.

- Possibility Thinkers see competition as a stimulus.
- Impossibility Thinkers see competition as a strain.
- Possibility Thinkers see competition as a challenge.
- Impossibility Thinkers see competition as an obstacle.
- Possibility Thinkers see competition as a healthy sweat.
- Impossibility Thinkers see competition as a dangerous threat.
- Possibility Thinkers tend to react by thinking big or bigger than their competition.
- Impossibility Thinkers tend to react by shrinking back and withdrawing from the action.

How you react to competition may explain where you are today, where you are headed, and where you will eventually arrive.

While impossibility thinkers fear competition, Supersuccessful People welcome the challenge. Like the small businessman whose clothing store was threatened with extinction when a national chain store moved in and acquired all the properties on his block. This one particular businessman refused to sell. "All right then, we'll build all around you and put you out of business," the new competitors said. The day came when the small merchant found himself hemmed in with a new department store stretching out on both sides of his little retail shop. The competitors now opened shop. Their banners unfurled, "Grand Opening!" The merchant countered positively. He flew his own banner across the entire width of his store. It read, "Main Entrance."

How we react to competition shapes our careers, our characters, and our relationships with people. It determines what friends we choose, the dreams we pursue, the energy we command and consume, and—in a word—whether life will be heaven or hell.

How do you handle competition? Let's go back to the beginning of childhood for some clues. When a new child comes into this world, he automatically becomes a competitor for his own survival. He literally competes against the forces of death itself. His first anguished cry is uttered in a desperate call for security against new forces that would threaten him. During the first year of his life he competes against an environment that he instinctively understands threatens his existence.

The process never ends. As the child continues to grow, he encounters a steady stream of competitive experiences. Soon he meets another toddler who has the annoying habit of wanting the same toy or doll. How the child learns to deal with that situation may influence his decisions the rest of his life.

As early as two or three years of age, the child becomes aware of his or her genitals and begins to sense that there is around him a big boy and a big girl he calls daddy and mama. Now competition reaches a new level. How he responds to and relates competitively to these overpowering larger images of himself further determines how competition will be handled in later years.

A little child of four may be sitting at the table at dinnertime, jabbering away to his mother. Just then, father comes home from work and is anxious to tell mother something. So he says to the child, "Will you please be quiet and let me talk?" Or he may impatiently say in less kind words and tone, "Shut up and let me talk to your mother!" What's happening? The little child is being given a life-forming experience in competition.

The child, subjected to competition-threatening experiences, quickly learns that there are several alternatives. One is to become a withdrawn and shy person—"Somebody is always telling me to shut up, so I will!" Another is to decide that success isn't worth the effort because success calls for competition. Competition may appear to be a threatening and hostile experience to be avoided. On the other hand, the child may choose to react positively, facing the competition with a determination to win. A positive life-style is then fixed.

As soon as a child reaches school age, competition rears its—sometimes ugly—head again. Not only is there competition with classmates and playmates, but the child must also compete for the attention of the teacher. If he doesn't receive adequate emotional nourishment at home in preparation for this outside experience, he probably will do some ridiculous things in school just to win in the competition for attention that he falsely equates with affection. Some people only realize too late that attention is not the same thing as affection.

Competition is what makes adolescence so difficult. For it is then that a young person begins to realize his individuality, and that maturity means standing on one's own feet. But once again, the competitive world is threatening. So what happens? The teen-ager may choose what appears to be security and become a conformist. Conformity is, after all, a cop-out in the face of competition.

When there are several children in a given family, there is another form of competition. Some interesting studies have shown that where there are children, the oldest often has the most difficult time in making a mature adjustment to the social forces around him. He is always paving the road ahead, breaking ground for the other siblings. The youngest, on the other hand, often has the greatest drive, because he tends to fear competition less. And the middle child gets it from both ends, with competition coming from top and bottom.

Many a marriage collapses when a husband feels his wife is competing for salary or status. In a happy marriage the competition inherent in courtship gives way to a commitment. When two people love each other they stop competing and start caring. Courtship is a careful game that people play to

determine whether they want to keep competing or whether
they want to call an end to the competition and declare a beginning to a lifetime of caring, "for better or for worse, for
richer or for poorer, in sickness or in health, till death do
us part."

Of course, that's easier said than done. A woman once wrote
me to share her own experience with competition in marriage. She said, "I happen to be a very smart and successful
businesswoman. My husband's business wasn't doing too well
and I began to help him. I moved into the office and everything started improving. In fact, we started making a lot of
money. Suddenly my husband began to resent me. And as
soon as I was in the office, he became angry. I didn't realize
it until he threatened to pack up and leave. I asked him, 'What
have I done? I've been such a help to you. I wasn't even on
the payroll. I found my joy in watching the business succeed.'
And he said, 'Well, you are trying to tell me how to run my
business.' I told him I was sorry and that I didn't mean to.
I stopped going into the office and the business started going
down. His pride wouldn't allow him to say anything, but when
I asked if I could help, he said, 'Well, if you could come in
Thursday there's a lot of work.' So I started coming back in
and things started going up, until finally I was in there every
day again and the business was going great. Suddenly, without warning, my husband left me.

"I found him," she wrote me, "and we both said we were
sorry. So he's home now. But I don't know how the business
is going to be resolved or if I can actually be a part of it any
more. But I know one thing: I have changed. Something of
that old competitive instinct in me has been altered and I sense

and believe it is for the better. I have peace I have never known before in my life."

How do you handle competition? Psychological theory and practice divides on the way that question is answered. Some psychologists tend to be anticompetitive in their counsel, fearing that competition produces the threat of failure and subsequent neuroticism. Others contend that competition is important, that it adds meaning to life. Tension can be creative. It can be an uplifting force. Psychological systems divide on this issue.

Attitudes toward competition shape economic philosophy and practice also. There are economic systems in the world today that claim competition is evil because it puts some people down. In theory, the proponents of anticompetition economic systems say that everybody could be treated fairly by removing competition from the marketplace.

By contrast, the kind of economic system we have in the United States feeds on competition. Supporting our system is the belief that if competition is viewed creatively and positively, it will result in a dynamic challenge rather than a threat. It will bring greatness out in otherwise mediocre people. It will produce drive, energy, ambition, and enthusiasm. And if the spirit of Jesus Christ has control over our competition, then we will rise to the top by lifting people up. Everybody benefits if we learn to handle competition creatively.

But sometimes we don't. An executive vice-president of one of the top American enterprises once told me that he had suddenly lost his drive and ambition. He couldn't understand it, until he was helped to see that he felt threatened by another young executive who had recently been brought into the company. Now he was afraid that he would not reach the top post himself, would never become the chief executive or chairman of the board. To protect himself from imagined failure, he reacted to this new fanciful threat emotionally, "Okay, I don't want to lose in a power struggle. Therefore, I'll just retire."

He had copped out. He was so afraid of failure that he backed away from the competition. He would leave the company consoling his wounded ego: "Well, at least I rose to the level of executive vice-president." He really failed, however, because he saw competition as a threat instead of a positive challenge.

How do you handle competition? Here are some negative options that many people choose:

1. You can cop out and say, "I'm going to avoid all competitive situations." You can do that, but then you will live only half a life. You will never run the race, and so you will never lose. What distorted logic! You will never win, either.

2. You can look upon competition as a threatening experience. If you have a weak ego, you will attack your competition in a hostile, mean, and angry manner, or stew and turn out to be like catty people in an office coffee shop, putting their competition down. Or you will play the old jealousy game. Jealousy is nothing more than a negative reaction to a competitive situation. If you have problems with jealousy, you know that you haven't learned how to handle competition creatively. And you can become downright vindictive.

3. You can lose your individuality and get lost in the crowd. You will never, of course, be a free person. You will be an object carried along by forces and faces that really don't care for you. That's sure failure.

How to Compete Positively

How can you compete positively? There are two faith-building, life-changing ways to creatively handle competition.

1. YOU CAN COMPETE AGAINST YOURSELF

Do that and you can't lose. Begin by competing against what you did last year. To young ministers burning with ambition, I give this advice: Find a place where there are hundreds of thousands of people who are hurting. Dedicate yourself to that one place. Each year do a little better than you did last year. And in twenty years you will be shocked at what you have accomplished. In this way, none of your emotional energies will be drained in negative feelings—jealousy, criticism, complaints—all of which can easily dissipate your creative potential. Instead, the full force of your personality will be positively charged and constructively released, and you will end up successful and happy.

So be smart! Compete against yourself. Run against your fastest time. Jump against your highest mark. Win against yourself. Do this, and you will not resent, resist, or react negatively when you feel the tension of competition rising within you.

Competition pangs, like hunger, are built-in signals that God is trying to say something to you. When your appetite for attention, recognition, affection, food, security, and material needs increases, be sure to know that competition for satisfaction reaches a crisis stage. It is all-important, now, to keep a Positive Possibility Thinking attitude.

Respect competition, knowing that there is no gain without strain. Thank God for the competition that causes you to strain to grow. Keep your heart fixed on Christ's Spirit, remembering that competition need not be a threat nor stand in your way of becoming a Supersuccessful person—unless you allow it to wound your self-esteem. For "Supersuccess is building self-esteem in yourself and others through service."

When Christ's Spirit controls your drive and your ambition, you will be compulsively driven to ministry—to outdo yourself in helping people who are hurting. And in the process your self-esteem is fed through services to others who need the best you have to offer. So know that you are your own greatest competitor.

2. YOU CAN COMPETE AGAINST UNFINISHED TASKS

A TV interviewer once asked me, "Isn't your supersuccess in danger of becoming a big numbers game? You are on over 100 television stations, you have over 8,000 members in your church. You have written eleven books," and so forth.

My answer was immediate. "I take my cue from the unfinished tasks," I said. "If I were a doctor with vaccine to innoculate the children in a village against polio, I wouldn't count how many I have innoculated. I would only concern myself with how many more needed to be innoculated."

If you are in a business, don't look at what you have already done, or how big your competitor is. Rather, look at the untouched, untapped, and undeveloped market around you. Move upward and onward, always doing a little better than you did last year. That's competing against yourself. That's also competing against the unfinished task.

I was in theological school when I first came up against the harsh reality of competition. I had an enormous drive to do something great with the one life I had to live, a fact that quite naturally led me to the ministry, and to dream about being a pastor, some day, of one of the largest churches in America. But how would I do that? If I started my professional life by aiming secretly for such an ambitious position, I could run into serious trouble. I might be tempted to compromise in order to "impress the right people." I might be tempted to jealousy if someone else was offered the position I really wanted. I could see myself going into a whole life-long experience of inner conflict, compromise, and contradiction. It was to be a decisive moment in my life. For at that time I was given an assignment to write a paper on a minister named George Truitt. I had never heard of him. But I soon found that he graduated from seminary with the dream of spending his one life in one place and to do something great. So he took a small church in Dallas, Texas, and spent his entire ministry there—over forty years. When he ended his ministry, his church, the First Baptist Church, was the largest and by most standards the best church in his denomination.

Right then I knew I had my answer. I prayed, "Lead me, Lord, into a community where there will be so many spiritually hungry and hurting people that I can spend my whole life in one place and make it great. You only know, Lord, how big a job I can handle. Let the work grow as large as I am capable of handling."

So at the age of twenty-eight, I found myself in a denomination, the Reformed Church in America, which included the super-huge 4,000-member Marble Collegiate Church headed by Norman Vincent Peale. At that age, I was invited to move to California to begin a new church from scratch. That was the answer to my prayers. I decided then and there that if I spent forty years in this new church and if it grew by 100 members a year, our denomination could have not only a 4,000 member church in New York, but another Positive Thinking Center with 4,000 members on the Pacific Coast.

As I write this book, I am fifty years old. The church here in Garden Grove is twenty-two years old. There are now over 8,000 members, and we are still growing. And that's the way it should be, for there are still nearly 500,000 people living in a fifteen-mile radius of our church who are not active members of any organized religion. So we keep on competing against our own record, setting our goals each year based on the unfinished task around us.

Keep Practicing Possibility Thinking

There is no better way to face the challenges of competition than through the constant use of Possibility Thinking. With this mental process at work, you will discover several options:

1. You will be challenged by your competition to think bigger and better than ever before. In this way, competition becomes your friend. Without it, you become too comfortable and neglect people's needs. "Woe to those who are at ease in Zion."

2. "If you can't beat them, join them," a famous baseball player said as he switched teams. More than one competitive firm has found it significantly helpful to merge with their competitors. Do you eliminate your competition if you merge?

3. Face your competition with prayer. A friend once asked,

"What shall I pray?" I suggested, "Lord, let my competitors succeed or fail as you want them to!" He came back in a few days, enthusiastic, excited, and had this testimony: "That prayer performed a miracle," he said. "If my competitor succeeds, I'll know it's because God wants him to succeed."

I promise you this. If you keep a Possibility Thinking attitude, competition will be handled creatively. And if you can handle competition, you can handle your other problems with equal aplomb.

11 Enthusiasm – God's Beautiful Gift to You

The great way of living does not mean living without problems. All Supersuccessful People have problems. Their secret lies in how to turn their problems into enthusiasm-generating possibilities. Problems give meaning to life. Eliminate problems and life loses its creative tension. The problem of mass ignorance gives meaning to education. The problem of ill health gives meaning to medicine. The problem of social disorder gives meaning to government. The problem of sin gives meaning to religion.

If you employ Possibility Thinking perspectives, problems are not going to be eliminated. Not at all! Set a goal, as Supersuccessful People do, and you immediately create a new area of conflict. With every new goal, new problems arise. But that's good! Growth comes through a creative attitude toward problems. Every problem should be understood as a plus sign. Each gives meaning to life. That's the Possibility Thinking perspective. So tackle your problems enthusiastically, because the problem-solving process is an enthusiasm-generating activity. Enthusiasm is God's beautiful gift to you.

Some years ago I wrote a little story to try to capture the meaning of this great power:

WHAT IS ENTHUSIASM?

Enthusiasm Is That Mysterious Something that Turns an Average Person into an Outstanding Individual . . .

It lifts us from fatigue to energy. It pulls us up from mediocrity to excellence. It turns on a bright light in our life until our face glows and our eyes sparkle. It's a spiritual magnet that draws happy people to us. It's a joyful fountain that bubbles and causes people to come to our side and share their joy. Out of this fountain there leaps self-confidence that shouts to the world. "I can! It's possible! Let's go!" Enthusiasm is the long-sought-after fountain of youth. When old men stop to drink of its elixir, they suddenly dream new dreams, and mysterious energy surges through the body that moments before was fatigued, weary, and old. It's a source of energy that never runs out. Drink from this fountain of enthusiasm, and you will experience a miracle. Discouragement will fade away like the morning's fog in the noonday sun. Suddenly, you start laughing, whistling, singing, and you know you are a child of God. Enthusiasm—when someone offers it to you, take it, especially if you don't want it . . .

Now that's a great way to live. Show me a person who is enthusiastic, and I will show you a person who has a dream, a plan, a project or a goal aimed at solving some problem. And if that person makes God the center of his goal, there can be no defeat, no room for discouragement nor pessimism. So remember the words of Jesus in your goal setting: *"Seek ye first the kingdom of God, and his righteousness, and all these things shall be added unto you"* (Matt. 6:33).

Put a soul in your goal, approach your goal with God-given enthusiasm and you will not fail. Do I mean that life will be all roses for you? No, there will be dark days, days when you feel that you are at a low ebb. Dr. Felding Osbund, head of the Sociology Department at the University of Chicago, knew this when he said: "The human race moves in cycles, up and down, in a rhythm. A natural trend is for a society to go down. It continues to decline until it reaches a point beyond which it is not allowed to go, at which time it starts to pull up again, when an Eternal Force enters the scene. Some may want to call it God. Many have, but all I can say is that at a historical low ebb this Force produces a man or a movement which catches fire, and the upward cycle begins."

I call this Eternal Force God. That's why I am an unconquerable optimist. This is the root of my enthusiasm-generating faith. So when you see things going down, you know that it's simply the pendulum swinging down on its way toward swinging back up. Because there's an outside force that will not let it go too far.

This is the Possibility Thinking Perspective that turns problems into projects that produce enthusiasm. That's a great way to live. Even negative situations will positively excite you because you will look for positive opportunities in these problems.

Here is an example of what I mean. In recent years we have been facing an energy crisis. Now it is easy to spend one's time being negative about that. Energy specialists produce charts and tables that predict a gloomy future. But let's look at the bright side and see the possibilities in this crisis. One is that we are now compelled to drive our automobiles at more than fifty-five miles per hour. Think of the good that comes from that. Not only do we save some of our precious energy, but we save lives.

Let's imagine that two cars collide on the freeway. One spins off on the side. The ambulances come, and patrol cars charge up with red lights flashing. They lift the bodies out, and they are still alive. One little boy is only four years old. He's bleeding, crying, and badly hurt. He is rushed to the hospital where he is treated. His injuries are a broken leg and superficial wounds on his body. In a few days he is home. A patrolman reports, "Thank God the car was going only fifty-five. If that accident had happened at sixty-five miles an hour, that boy would be dead." The boy lived, and forty years from now he may be one of our country's great leaders.

That's what I mean by being enthusiastic about problems. Because of the energy shortage, we have to drive slower and perhaps less. We will never know what the benefits are. Perhaps, because we are no longer allowed to use the automobile in the old way, families will spend more time together. Maybe church attendance will improve. I know that lives are going to be saved on the freeway. When you believe in God, it's easy to believe that what looks like a problem is going to turn out to be a blessing.

Four Options in the Face of Problems

In the face of problems, you have four options. Two are positive; two are negative.

Consider first the negative options when a problem hits you:

DECIDE TO CONSENT TO IT

...t, and accept defeat. That's tempting. I
...ally when you have prayed and practiced Pos-
...y Thinking, and you still can't resolve your problems.
But if you give in, surrender, and consent to your problem,
look what will happen! Everything will get darker, your road
will be paved with catastrophe. The will to die will be so strong
that you may consider suicide.

But what if you have been praying and practicing Possibility Thinking, and you are still in a bad strait? All I can say
is that you would be much worse off than you are. If you
keep on keeping on and the problem isn't resolved, at least
you will change. You will have been a courageous inspiration to those around you. In addition, when you change, your
problem will begin to change for the better also.

When facing a problem, your first option is to *consent* to
it, but that makes no sense because of what it does to you.

2. YOU CAN RESENT IT

Many people choose this second negative option. But if you
choose to resent your problem, you will become a tough, hard,
cold, and bitter person. You will feel sorry for yourself. You
will think the world is against you; that God has abandoned
you; that your friends don't understand you; that nobody loves
you. And then you will be where anyone possessed by self-
pity winds up—lonely, isolated, and unloved, at the end of
the road. The reason you will not be surrounded by love is
because you, in your self-pity, will have driven your friends

away. Your only companions will be mutually negative people, who require the morbid company of like-minded cynical complainers.

My cab driver wanted to talk. He was a hard and cynical man. In fact, I couldn't begin to use the language that he used while talking about his problems. When I asked a few questions to discover the reason for his bitterness, he told of two marriages that hadn't worked out, and of his living with another woman with whom he had troubles. He was nearly sixty years old and one of the most miserable people I have ever met.

Why had he turned into a cold and bitter human being? It was obvious from what he told me that he had reacted to his first divorce with anger. That was the only response he knew, and for forty years or more he had been practicing this response to any and every problem that arose. But look how counterproductive that habitual response is! What did he gain by it! All his anger achieved was to deepen his own sense of failure and to repel attractive and potentially helpful people. That's why resentment is the most destructive attitude to harbor in response to problems.

Now let's look at the other pair of options, which Supersuccessful People use in their enthusiasm to turn problems into projects.

1. YOU CAN INVENT SOLUTIONS
TO THE PROBLEMS YOU FACE

Inventing solutions is what we mean by Possibility Thinking. How do you do that? First of all, by believing that any problem can be turned into a positive experience. Once you start thinking in these terms, you will generate the enthusiasm you need to move ahead.

Once a railway express clerk by the name of Sears, living near Redwood Falls, Minnesota, received a box of watches that had been sent to a jeweler in this town. The jeweler refused to accept the shipment. Meanwhile the distributor in Chicago said he didn't want them back because the shipping charges would be too expensive. Instead, he made an offer to the railway express clerk. "You can have them for $2 each," the distributor said. So what did the man do? He turned his problem into an opportunity. He simply put together a catalog with some pictures of watches, and sent it around to other railway clerks. He was so successful that he ordered more watches and enlarged his catalog. That was the start of the Sears Roebuck catalog.

Some of the greatest humanitarian enterprises in the United States were started and succeeded because of some Possibility Thinkers' enthusiastic responses to problems that appeared to be insurmountable.

A hopeless old drunk was brought into a New York City hospital. "You know, this is your fiftieth visit," said the admitting doctor. The old man considered that information for a moment and replied, "I think that calls for a celebration." The doctor shook his head in despair, and said, "I can't give you a drink. You know that." The old drunk muttered, "I'm hopeless; right, doc?" The doctor said, "I'll tell you what I will do. We have just brought a young man in, nineteen or twenty years old. This is his first time. I want you to go and pay him a visit. Take a good look at him, and have him take a good look at you. Maybe he won't take the road you have taken."

The old alcoholic was shocked at this and exclaimed, "You mean you will give me a drink if I do that!" "Sure," said the doctor. "You do that and I'll get you a drink." So the old man went down the hall and found a clean-cut young man who was at the turning point of his own life. "You know, boy," said the old man, "you don't want to turn out the way I did. I was young like you once. I had a mother who had dreams for me. And I had dreams. Now look at me."

Then something happened inside the old man. The more he talked to the young fellow, the more he discovered that he had a mission in life. He had to save that boy! They talked all morning, and finally they made a promise. The old man said, "I'll tell you what I will do. If you ever need a drink, you call me, okay?" And the boy said, "I'll do the same for you."

That was the turning point for the old man. He went on to become the founder of Alcoholics Anonymous, all because he shared his life to save another. He had found an inner power that you and I know to be the power of God. He had faced his own problem, invented a solution, and gone on to help millions of others.

Easy? No, not at all. Possibility Thinking is never easy. It calls for tough-minded patience. But never underestimate the power of patience. On your way to inventing solutions, you may wear your problem out. But there's more. Patience also helps you stretch your thinking. These impossible problems you face! Do you know what they are? They are designed by God to challenge you to accept bigger problems, and to invent even greater solutions. Keep looking for the possibilities in the problems that overwhelm you. God does not give up on you and you are not to give up on your problems. How do you keep that patience alive? There are some inspired words in Psalms 84:5–7 that can help you:

"Blessed are those who dwell in thy house, ever
singing thy praise!
Blessed are the men whose strength is in thee,
in whose heart are the highways to Zion
As they go through the valley of Baca [*trouble*]
they make it a place of springs . . .
They go from strength to strength."

The word "Baca" comes from the Hebrew, which means "to weep." The same root word is used to describe the balsam tree, which is called the weeping tree because of the gumlike sap that oozes forth when it is cut. The sap bubbles forth and literally heals the wound. So it is that there are some people who go through troubled times, through the Valley of Weeping, and turn their experiences into life-giving, healing experiences. They turn their problems into possibilities. That's being a Supersuccess.

The Pool of Bethesda is the setting for one of Thornton Wilder's plays. According to the Biblical story, whenever the water rippled, the first person to step into the pool was healed. But in Wilder's handling of this story, one sick person was himself a physician and in need of healing. As he approached, the poolkeeper offered this admonition: "Draw back, physician—healing is not for thee. Without your wound, where would your power be? It is your very sorrow that puts kindness in your face and makes your low voice tremble into the hearts of men. Angels themselves cannot heal the wretched as can one human being broken on the wheel of life." *In love's service only wounded will be accepted.*

Enthusiastic people always keep on believing that some things will work out. In one way or another they manage to succeed. Along the way they run into people who believe in them. (People aren't going to believe in you if you keep telling them that you can't do it.) Secure people attract other secure people. Support comes to them in unexpected times and ways and from unexpected sources because they keep believing in their own possibilities.

Clark Eddy, a teacher of music in Schenectady, New York, tells this story about one of his students:

Barbara, a fourth-grade girl, came to him and was determined to play in the school marching band. She had the lips to blow a horn and she passed in a rhythm test, but she had one serious difficulty. On her tiny hands there were no fingers. Just the beginning of stubs and the digit of one thumb. That was all.

But Barbara was determined. So Mr. Eddy borrowed a mellophone and began to teach her how to play. Hour after hour she struggled until she began to play the horn faultlessly. She learned how to manipulate the valves with the little humps and bumps that were her substitute for fingers. And when it came time to join the marching band, she marched in perfect rhythm. Few people along the parade route knew that she had no fingers, and that, under her marching uniform, was a twisted leg and deformed foot without toes.

"God doesn't sponsor flops." God doesn't make any mistakes. *We make mistakes,* when we cut ourselves off from God's miracle-working power by our negative thinking. Keep on thinking possibilities and you will come up with a solution to your impossible problem also.

2. YOU CAN PREVENT NEEDLESS
PROBLEMS FROM OCCURRING

By preventing problems from occurring, I do not mean that you should set your goals so low that you will never have to face difficulties. In pursuing your goals, you should set your standards high enough to be challenging. Problems are often a complement to your courage.

A college student once complained to me that he was having a difficult time with his physics course. He said, "What if I fail, I will feel so stupid!" I replied, "On the contrary. You could have sailed through college taking snap courses. Instead, you chose to struggle through one of the hardest courses in the whole college curriculum. The very fact that you are having trouble is a compliment to you. You had the nerve to try."

Keep your standards high. Try the impossible. Then learn how to *prevent* problems. What do I mean?

- Expect difficulties, obstacles and problems every time you set a goal. Every new commitment will create new areas of conflict.
- Probe, inquire, and seek the wisest advice you can get from experienced people to determine in advance what problems you can expect and whether they can be prevented in part, in whole, or in intensity by advance knowledge and preparation. Ask people wiser than yourself, "Is there anything wrong with my plan?" Then listen and avoid needless problems.
- Learn from every mistake. Take each error and let it turn you into a wiser person. In that way you will draw dividends from your difficulties.

• Obey the natural, spiritual, and moral laws. If you follow these laws, they will help prevent problems. If you ignore them, they will break you.

So many problems come to us because we violate natural laws. We don't eat right, exercise right, or sleep right. We drink too much, smoke too much, or eat too much. So problems are inevitable. Your efficiency, effectiveness, and creativity is lowered. You cannot be a Supersuccess if you disregard these natural laws.

Ignoring spiritual laws takes its toll also. Spiritual laws require that you feed your mind on dynamic faith every week. If you come to church once a month, it's not enough. The human soul has an inspirational tank that only holds a seven-day supply. And unless we are coasting downhill, your enthusiasm generating motor will start sputtering as soon as it reaches the smallest hill.

Then there are the moral laws. The Ten Commandments: "Thou shalt not kill!" "Thou shalt not commit adultery!" "Thou shalt not steal!" If you decide you no longer have to live by these laws and feel they are outdated, you are headed for certain trouble. This is not an unfriendly threat. It is a friendly warning. Live by these laws and you will prevent the biggest kind of problems from attacking you. Break them and they will break you.

Keep Communication Lines with God Open

My final word to you then, on facing problems, is to make sure your lines of communication with God are clear, clean, and open. Weekly church attendance and daily prayers and meditations will keep you in tune with God. You'll find the faith to face frustrating problems with a creative Possibility Thinking attitude.

Many years ago, in England, the most famous elephant in the circus world was an elephant named Bozo. Bozo was a beautiful beast—a great big tender hunk of gentleness. Children would come to the circus and extend their chubby open palms, filled with peanuts, through the gate, and the elephant, with tender eyes, would drop his trunk with a nibbling, mobile nose, would pick up the peanuts out of their hands and curl his trunk and feed himself, and almost smile as he swallowed the gift. Everyone loved Bozo.

Then one day something happened that changed his personality from positive to negative almost overnight. One day he almost stampeded, threatening to crush the man who was cleaning his cage. Then he began to charge the children. The circus owner knew the elephant was now dangerous and that the problem had to be faced. He came to the conclusion that he would have to exterminate this big old beast. This decision hurt him, first, because he loved the elephant; second, because it was the only elephant he had. Bozo had been imported from India, and it would cost him thousands of pounds to replace him.

Then he got an idea. This desperate and crude man decided that he would sell tickets to view the execution of Bozo. At least he would be able to raise the money to replace him.

The story spread, tickets were sold out, and the place was jammed. There, on the appointed date, was Bozo in his cage, as three men with high-powered rifles rose to take aim at the great beast's head.

Just before the signal to shoot, a little stubby man with a brown derby hat stepped out of the crowd, walked over to the owner and said, "Sir, this is not necessary. This is not a bad elephant." The owner said, "But it is. We must kill him before he kills someone." The little man with the derby hat said, "Sir, give me two minutes alone in his cage, and I'll prove that you are wrong. He is not a bad elephant."

The circus owner thought for a moment, wrung his hands and said, "All right. But first you must sign a note absolving me of all responsibility if you get killed."

The little man scribbled on a piece of paper the words, "I absolve you of all guilt," signed his name, folded the paper and handed it to the circus owner. The owner opened the door to the cage. The little man threw his brown derby hat on the ground and stepped into the cage. As soon as he was inside, the door was locked behind him. The elephant raised his trunk, bellowed and trumpeted loudly.

But before the elephant could charge, the little man began talking to him, looking him straight in the eye. The people close by could hear the little man talking, but they couldn't understand what he was saying. It seemed as if he was speaking in an unknown tongue. The elephant still trembled, but hearing these strange words from this little man he began to whine, cry, and wave his head back and forth. Now the stranger walked up to Bozo and began to stroke his trunk. The now gentle beast tenderly wrapped his trunk around the feet of the little man, lifted him up, carried him around his cage and cautiously put him back down at the door. Everyone applauded.

As he walked out of the cage, the little man said to the keeper, "You see? He *is* a good elephant. His only problem is that he is an Indian elephant, and he only understands Hindustani. He was homesick for someone who could understand him. I suggest, sir, that you find someone in London who speaks Hindustani, and have him come in and just talk to the elephant. You'll have no problems."

As the man picked up his derby and walked away, the circus owner looked at the note and read the signature of the man who had signed it. The man with the little brown derby was Rudyard Kipling.

People also become frustrated, angry, and defeated when no one understands them. If you are frustrated and tempted to become angry when you're facing a problem, and tempted to react negatively, *check* your communication lines with God. He understands. He speaks your language.

God *believes* in you! God understands your fears, hurts, heartaches, and problems. Draw close to him.

He'll show you his plan on how you, too, can turn your problems into possibilities!

12 Turn Your Mountains into Miracles

Let's check your progress.

- You have set new goals for yourself.
- You have discovered new problems inherent within these goals.
- You believe these problems are now actually slumbering possibilities, sleeping giants.
- You are well on your way toward becoming a Supersuccessful person.

Now what happens? There will be times when your forward momentum will be throttled by obstructions, delays, and unfulfilled expectations. You may not be unlike the bird I once saw as I was riding through a canyon. The bird was beating his wings and flying for dear life, but he was not moving ahead. He was holding his spot against the wind.

How do you handle frustration? Supersuccessful People naturally keep looking for possibilities. They don't allow themselves to become defeated and discouraged in times of difficulties. They know that their biggest dreams seem impossible simply because they are *big*. And they know that on the way toward achieving the realization of their dreams they can expect to experience frustration. But that doesn't scare them off. *For they know that frustration is God's opportunity to shape, mold, humble, mature, and guide them along the way.*

In my own frustrations, I have been helped enormously by remembering these words: "Fret not yourself because of the wicked. . . . Trust in the Lord, and do good" (Psalm 37:1–3, RSV).

There are two kinds of people in the world. There are people who cannot take the heat. And there are people who will not accept defeat. The second, because they refuse to accept defeat, discover that mountains are miracles waiting to be uncovered. You can turn your mountains into miracles. How is that possible?

A Tough Faith for Rough Times

Begin by building a close, comforting relationship with God and trust him. In the biblical story of Job, God allowed all of Job's possessions to be taken away in order to test this pious man's faith. With his children gone, his health broken, his riches depleted, this once wealthy man sits now on an ash heap, with sores covering his body. What does he do? He turns his mountain into a miracle. The miracle is his decision to react positively – helpfully – optimistically – instead of cynically, negatively, and pessimistically. "Surely God will not do wickedly" (Job 34:12).

Job's response gives us the basis on which we can build a tough faith for rough times. Believe that God is the ultimate judge of your life, and that he will not allow any problem to come to you that cannot (with Possibility Thinking) become a learning, a turning, or an earning experience. Believe this and you will become the kind of person who will not accept defeat. You will meet the heat and live victoriously.

Not long ago I read the story of Mother Cabrini. She was the youngest of thirteen children, born to a poor family in Northern Italy. Her parents died when she was two. And at the age of eight she announced, "I am going to be a missionary to China when I grow up." Her brothers and sisters laughed at her. "You can't be a missionary," they said. "The church only uses men, not women. Anyway, you are too sickly." But she was determined, and when she finished her formal education, which would have qualified her to become a teacher in an order, the Catholic Church refused to take her. "You are too weak," they said.

And she was. She didn't even weigh a hundred pounds, and she spit blood all the time. But her strong will overcompensated for her weak body. "I'll take my case to the Pope," she declared.

"Sister Cabrini," The Pope's voice was firm as he looked down on this frail, determined nun, "the church does not send women to be missionaries to China or any place." "Then, Holy Father," she responded, "I shall start an order for women only."

"Agreed," the Pope returned, "providing you will go as a missionary to Italians in New York City." Sister Frances Cabrini accepted the compromise.

For months she waited on Ellis Island, still spitting blood. Finally, frustrated with the senseless delay, she appealed to the hierarchy of the Catholic Church in New York. "Frankly, Sister," she was told, "You're too sickly. Go home!" Righteously indignant, she stamped her foot and rebuked the Archbishop. "Sir, I will not go home. I am at home here now." With that, the Archbishop gave in and let her stay.

Few people today know what New York was like at the turn of the century. Poor and homeless immigrants were wandering lonely, unloved, and lost in a new land. To them came this angel from God, and by 1916, through her beautiful love, over sixty houses had been founded, providing homes for the orphans and hospitals for the sick and the dying.

Trust God. He may not want you to go to China. He may want you to go to New York. He may frustrate your dream, but he will not leave you without dreams. He will give you new opportunities. He may trouble you. Sometimes he will test you. And sometimes the circumstances will seem intolerable, but you will find that God has only turned you toward a more fruitful ministry, like Mother Cabrini.

No one escapes trouble. But it is not what happens to you that counts. It's how you react to trouble that makes all the difference. Trouble never leaves you where it found you, but changes you into either a bitter person or a better person. And the exciting truth is, no one can remove your freedom to choose how you will react in the face of frustration. You can take a negative attitude or a positive attitude.

You Can Master Your Frustrations

When you are faced with frustrations, and you can't seem to climb the mountain, there is one thing you can do. And there are several things you should not do. Let's look at these first:

1. DON'T <u>TAPE</u> YOUR FRUSTRATIONS

Many people record them, remember them, rehearse them. They tell everybody how frustrated they are and how they have been hurt. Years later they demonstrate the amazing ability to recall all the details. They harbor the negative memories. Why? Do they fear loneliness if they forsake these past hurts and frustrations with whom they have kept morbid, destructive, mental company all along?

2. DON'T <u>SCRAPE</u> THEM

Frustrations are like mosquito bites. Scratch them and you increase the itch and prolong the effect of the bite.

One of my favorite stories is about a woman on a bus who was loudly and rudely spouting off. Her behavior was crude and abusive. When she was about to leave the bus, the driver said, "Madam, you left something behind." She turned and grumbled, "What did I leave behind?" And the driver said, gently, "A very bad impression."

3. DON'T <u>ESCAPE</u> THEM

In the face of frustration our first and natural inclination is to escape.

Dr. Butler of Baylor University said it. "When things get tough, don't move. People and pressures shift but the soil remains the same no matter where you go." If you can't live through this problem, you won't live through the next problem in the next place you plan to go. If you can't live through this frustration, you won't live through the next one, either. Yes, "People and pressures shift but the soil remains the same no matter where you go."

Remember this when you are tempted to escape your frustrations. *No frustration will ever enjoy eternal life. Every mountain has a top. Every hill has a crest.* Every difficulty is going to come to an end sometime. All you need is the power to keep climbing until you reach the top. Then and there you will catch the vision of what God had in mind for you all the time.

In periods of frustration you may feel that your problems will never leave you. The question is, who is going to give up and quit first, the frustration or you? That depends on your spirit.

We know from psychiatry that there exists in every human being the will to live and the will to die. When you are frustrated and can't climb the mountain, you want to quit, to give up, even to die. Never! Never! Never give up! Always let God make that decision. If you have a dream and you are frustrated and are ready to kill that great idea, don't do it! That's God's job. Only God has that power.

The former Israeli prime minister, Golda Meir, spoke of that spirit in a recent interview. She said, "All my country has is spirit. We don't have petroleum dollars. We don't have mines with great wealth in the ground. We don't have the support of a worldwide public opinion that looks favorably on us. All Israel has is the spirit of its people. And if the people lose their spirit, even the United States of America cannot save us."

Hang on. Have spirit. You will survive. Don't *tape* your frustrations. Don't *scrape* them. And don't try to *escape* them.

4. AND FINALLY, DON'T TRY TO <u>DRAPE</u> YOUR FRUSTRATIONS

You can't hide them. If you have feelings of frustration, they will come out.

You can bury a stone. You can bury a stick. You can bury an old tin can. But you can't bury a worm. What's the point? Simply that you cannot bury and repress negative emotions and feelings. They will worm their way back to the surface. And you are likely to blow your stack at the best people at the worst possible times.

Open Up or Blow Up

Don't try to hide and pretend there is nothing wrong. Develop the ability to open up before you blow up. Try, in a small, quiet meeting, to get to the persons who are the source of your frustration. Now open up. Try to be as kind and as Christian as you can be. If in your weakness you lack the patience and restraint to remain kind in the venting of your frustrations — apologize! But whatever you do, don't try to hide your negative feelings. Remember the wisdom of the Bible: "Do not let the sun go down on your anger" (Eph. 4:26, RSV).

It's no secret that difficulties, injustices, and unfairness abound in life. So what do you do? Here's the answer. *You shape your life by using these frustrations to lead you to a closer relationship with God.*

Let Your Frustrations Shape You

Handle the injustice and unfairness and the frustration building up within you by using what I call *Still Power*. The Psalmist said: "Be still, and know that I am God" (Psalms 46:10).

Go into meditation and prayer. And ask God, "Father, have I been right? Have I been clean? Have I given my job all that I should have given it? Have I treated others right? Am I part of the problem?" Listen to the still small voice of God and you will be surprised what you will hear.

Now check your relationship with God. Perhaps you are totally estranged from him. Obviously, you are not going to get power to overcome your frustrations until you reconcile your life with him.

Perhaps God is merely a friendly stranger to you. You respect everything you have heard about God, but you have no personal relationship with him. Perhaps yours is a nodding acquaintance, but you are certainly not on a first-name basis with him. What you need is a deep, warm, intimate friendship with God. Like two people who can cry together, laugh together, and talk long into the night. That kind of relationship with God is possible. He wants to be your close, intimate, personal friend. You can become such a friend when you accept Jesus Christ as your Savior, because he cleanses your sins, cleanses you of negative thoughts, and makes it possible for God's beautiful love to come into your life.

I know that God wants to be your closest personal friend. Ask him to forgive you and love you and guide you. He will. And then you will have *Still Power,* the kind of power you need to climb the mountain, to turn the mountain into a miracle. In the face of your personal mountain, you will not *mope* with despair. You will not *grope* your way blindly. You will not *dope* your mind with narcotics from a bottle, a box, or a bag. But you will *cope* with *hope* in your heart.

Discover that beautiful relationship with God and then you find that frustrations are shaping you into a better, bigger person.

A woman who had sustained major surgery asked her doctor, "Do you think I will ever walk again?" He looked her squarely in the eye and said, "That's the wrong question. It is not what I think. It's what you think. Do *you* think you will ever walk again?"

When God's presence comes into your life, you will begin to imagine that things are going to get better; that they are not going to stay the way they are. Such possibility thinking will actually cause your circumstances to improve. You will then contribute to the solution rather than to the problem.

So let your frustrations shape you. St. Paul wrote: "Those whom [the Lord] loves, he reproves and chastens." Because God really loves you, you will grow from your frustrations. He will teach you patience, control, humility, and restraint.

I met not long ago a dying young woman, who had become a Christian through my Hour of Power telecast. "Dr. Schuller," she said to me, "I don't know why I have lived as

long as I have. But I really believe there is a purpose for it.
I was frightened when I first learned that I had cancer. I was
so afraid that I would be a burden on my family and friends.
Then I heard you talk about possibilities in all adversities,
and I dared to believe that I could be an inspiration to my
people until my dying day. So every time someone comes
to see me, I pray, 'Lord, how can I minister to these friends
who care for me hour after hour?'" God is answering her
prayers. Everyone who helps her tells the same story. "I go
to help her and when I leave I have been helped by her."

This young woman is doing a beautiful job. She is no burden on her loved ones, nor on her family. She has been shaped
into a gorgeous and beautiful person who is an inspiration
to everyone who has the privilege of caring for her.

Let your frustrations shape you into a beautiful person.

And when you hit some low point and think that prayer
doesn't work, that God is not real, and your mountain is
insurmountable—then what do you do?

During a long conversation with Dr. Victor Frankl, the
Viennese psychiatrist mentioned earlier in this book, I asked
him, "How can I make people believe in God today?" I wanted
to know how, in the midst of despair and darkness, when
God seems totally absent, I could help a person believe that
God is shaping his life through the very frustrations he is experiencing. Dr. Frankl's reply went something like this:

"You are," he said, "like an actor on a stage. You are born
on stage and stay on stage until the end of life. The spotlight
is bright and it is on you. The houselights are dark. You cannot see the audience. There is only a black hole before you.
The audience sits in darkness and you do not hear or see

them. But you are very much aware of their presence judging you. This silent presence is also encouraging you and probably inspiring you. This awareness energizes you, motivates you, and guides you. It determines your behavior while on stage. And if you keep your mind on pleasing the unseen in the black hole, before you know it, the end comes. The lights go on and you see their faces. There is applause."

"In effect," Dr. Frankl concluded, "God is like a black hole. You cannot see his face. You cannot hear his voice, but you know there is a presence watching you who cares about your performance."

Is it possible that an all-wise God may send frustrations our way in order to protect us in ways we may never know? Frustrations may be God's miracles to guide us.

I sat next to a man at a banquet about a year ago who told me an amazing story:

Dr. Schuller, I believe in miracles. I pride myself on getting to work on time. If the telephone rings when I am ready to leave the house, I tell my wife to tell them I have already left. She always did, except for one morning. The phone rang and she said, "Oh, he's just getting ready to leave." I swore at her under my breath as I went to pick up the phone. Silently she said, "I'm sorry, I'm sorry." Of all people it was the one person I was trying to avoid. Now the guy had me cornered on the line. I couldn't cut him off because there were political involvements and I have would have been cutting my own throat. I just had to keep the guy happy on the other end of the line. Finally, I looked at my watch and said, "Oh, my God, I should be at work. I'm going to be late." If this guy hadn't held me up, I would have been on the bridge already, crossing over the freeway at the interchange, halfway there. At that point, my house shook, and the ground seemed like water. It was the big earth-quake of three years ago. I discovered later that the bridge over which I was to have been at that moment had collapsed.

•   •   •

We will never know what divine providence may lie behind our frustrations. On my first trip to the Soviet Union, I made secret arrangements to meet with a large gathering of Christians. The meeting was carefully arranged ahead of time. My instructions were to keep a low profile, and not to say or do anything unusual; or, I was warned, I would be followed by the KGB to the secret meeting place, and as a result the Christian leaders would be imprisoned.

A carefully laid out schedule was established. I would take a plane from Leningrad to Kiev, and would transfer to Luvov where I was to wait in a hotel lobby to be met by a leader of the underground church. The rendezvous would take place sometime between the hours of 9:00 and 11:00 A.M. the next morning. The underground pastor was under instructions not to wait beyond 11:00 A.M., or his loitering in the hotel lobby would be viewed with suspicion.

On the day before I was to join the underground Christians, I asked my guide to take me to see the Leningrad Museum of Atheism, where I was shocked to see a photograph of myself standing in the pulpit of my California church. Here also were photographs of Billy Graham, Martin Luther King, and the Pope. Obviously my guide now identified me! Seeing me in person gave him the inflated impression that I was not an ordinary tourist. I knew then that I would be followed, and that the trip to Luvov could be extremely hazardous. What really shook me up was that my plane was scheduled to leave for Kiev within two hours.

The questions began to burn in my mind: *"What do I do about tomorrow morning's rendezvous? Do I keep it, or don't I?* If I don't keep it, I may miss a great opportunity to inspire the church that will be meeting in secret. But if I keep this appointment, will I be followed? Will I endanger the lives of the secret believers?" The questions kept me worried. What decision would you have made? What would you have done? It was one of the most anxious and frustrating moments of my life. *Not because of what would happen to me, but because of what could happen to innocent believers.*

At four o'clock we boarded our plane in Leningrad and flew to Kiev. Here an Intourist guide was waiting to receive us and to assist us in transferring to another plane, which was to leave for Luvov in thirty-five minutes. The Intourist guide, without comment, promptly put us in a cab, said something to the driver, and sent us off.

My companion, Mr. Eichenberger, and I sat in the back, fully expecting to be driven to the next building. Instead, the cab headed out into the country! We passed through a grove of trees, and away from the airport! Since we had only thirty-five minutes between planes, I became uneasy. I said to Mr. Eichenberger, "I don't think we are headed for another airport. Perhaps we are being called in for interrogation." So we agreed on the answers we would give to their questions, if they interviewed us separately.

Suddenly we saw the skyscrapers of a city ahead of us. By now thirty minutes had passed! We knew we were not going to make a thirty-five minute plane transfer! The ride continued until it became pitch dark and our headlights pierced the darkness. At this point we approached an entrance to grounds that looked very formal. On either side of the road we saw the big red star which now we recognized to be the symbol of the Red Army. We therefore expected to be ushered into the headquarters of the Red Army. To our surprise, we discovered it to be an army airport.

Our cab driver stopped in front of a building and we were ordered upstairs and into a room. The door closed behind us. We were ordered to sit down. Military people paced up and down, chattering incessantly in Russian. Forty minutes passed. An hour passed. Two hours passed! Unable to hold back any longer, I spoke out, "We have to get to Luvov tonight!" I was insistent. No one understood me, so I drew a picture of a little train, with an arrow pointing from Kiev to Luvov. (It is amazing what you can do with pictures!) "Nyet, nyet," they said, meaning, "No, no."

Now, it was nearly midnight, and they finally realized how upset we were. (At that moment we discovered that in Russia if you can't get your way, you take off your shoe and pound the table with it! Since they don't want to get people upset, they'll do anything to keep up a good front!) So, in order to get us to calm down they found an English-speaking person who said, "You will not go to Luvov tonight. There is an unexpected thunderstorm. You can hear it thunder now! There are no planes or trains leaving. You will not go to Luvov tonight. We will put you in a hotel. Tomorrow morning we will put you on the first plane to Luvov. You will get to Luvov at 11:30 A.M. tomorrow!" We went to the hotel and the next morning we boarded our plane. We arrived in Luvov, and were at our hotel at 11:45, about forty-five minutes past the hour of our rendezvous! It was too late to meet our contact. The planned meeting was frustrated–I'm convinced–by God who was stepping in to reshape the plans we had carefully made.

For the interesting thing is that I have flown nearly a million miles and this was the only time I ever missed a flight where bad weather had caused the plane to be grounded! That happened on that Tuesday in Russia!

God kept the plane down to keep me from rendezvousing the next morning with the underground churchmen! For I didn't know until I got back to the hotel that I was spied upon by the KGB men. One of them was on the outside of the front door, another was on the outside of the side door, and still another one was posted right outside our door! This last one happened to be a woman. She logged us when we went into the room and she logged us when we went out! We were under constant surveillance for twenty-four hours, and we would certainly have led the underground church leaders to a prison cell.

I tell you, I believe in God! He does guide! He does lead! Give your soul that kind of a positive faith. It will keep you cool, calm, and collected when frustrations block your plans.

You are Supersuccessful if you have learned to handle competition and now frustration. That's maturity. Not even mountains can stop you now.

13 Recycle Your Energy for Energy Unlimited

Thomas Buston once wrote:

The longer I live, the more deeply I am convinced that what makes the difference between one man and another, the great and the insignificant, is energy, that invincible determination, a purpose once formed, nothing can take away. This energetic quality will do anything that is meant by God to be done in this world, and no talent, no training, no opportunity, no circumstance will make any man a man without it.

Ralph Waldo Emerson once put this thought more succinctly: "The world belongs to the energetic."

Supersuccessful People have energy unlimited because they know how to recycle energy.

How can you have unlimited energy? To answer that question, let's begin by discussing the major causes for fatigue.

1. FATIGUE COMES FROM HOARDING ENERGY

Some people are tired because they are *afraid* they are going to get tired. They don't spend their energy because they want to save it. And because they are not spending it, they are constantly fatigued.

I woke up this morning and it was still dark out of doors. When I noticed that it was only 5:00 A.M., I said to myself, "Boy, I'm still tired, and I won't go back to sleep now." (Notice the negative thought. If you think you won't go back to sleep, of course you won't.) Then a thought entered, "If I want energy, the best way to get it is to jump out of bed and get going." So I dressed in my running suit and prepared to take a long run.

Soon I was running off into the hills. Exactly sixty-five minutes after I started my uninterrupted run, I arrived at my front gate. I took a hot shower, and I could feel the blood in every inch of my skin. I was more energetic than ever. I had received energy by giving out energy.

So here's the principle: Dynamic exercise produces energy. You can't hoard it. We know from psychiatric observations that nine-tenths of all fatigue among sedentary people is psychological and emotional.

I am blessed by God with tremendous energy. But I don't think I am genetically richer in energy than other people. Here is my simple testimony. "In Him [meaning in God and in Christ] *we live* [are really alive] *and move* [instead of sitting down and slouching and sleeping lazily] *and have our being* (Acts 17:28). God is the cosmic source of all energy. And when

we are close to God and in tune with him, we tap the source
of energy.

2. FATIGUE COMES FROM BOREDOM

Every human being has conflicting needs: *security* and *stimulation.*

The trouble is, these needs often contradict each other. For
instance, if you seek "security" you will suffer boredom and,
hence, lack stimulation. If you achieve ultimate security, you
will achieve ultimate boredom. The only escape from fatigue-
producing boredom is to expose yourself to the energy-
producing stimulation of a risky adventure.

At a seminar I attended some time ago I heard someone
ask a doctor, "Why is it that some people have more energy
than others?" He replied, "It's largely a matter of glands. Some
people have energetic genes.' The speaker pointed out that
the endocrine glands are mostly responsible for rushing the
adrenalin into the blood, and this is what makes the difference. But I wasn't satisfied. I asked, "What stimulates the glands
to activate the adrenalin?" The doctor answered, "The difference is that some people's glands get stimulated and they put
out energy, while other people's glands don't get stimulated,
so they don't put out energy."

But that, obviously, wasn't much help, so I replied, "Then
it's more a matter of *blands* than glands." By that I meant bland
living—not spiced-up, not exciting, dull, mediocre, ho-hum.
Energy is more a matter of blands than it is of glands. As you
give out energy, more energy is fed back into you again. If
you give it out, it reproduces more within you.

That means there are two ways of expending energy. You

can waste it, or you can recycle it. When you are controlled by negative emotions, doubt, fear, worry, anger, hostility, self-pity and jealousy, you waste your energy. Vitality literally drains out of you.

Recycling energy is when you spend yourself building, constructing, helping, and pursuing great causes. In turn, you become more enthusiastic, which recycles your energy supply. And that's what we are going to learn to do—to develop a life-style that will guarantee a constant recycling of energy.

3. FATIGUE COMES FROM NOT HAVING A DREAM

Dare to dream and you begin to experience excitement that produces energy. Turn off your dreams and you will experience fatigue day and night.

When people cautiously try to avoid their problems and the problems of other people—when they don't want to make sacrifices, when they don't want to be unselfish, when they don't want to give, and start playing it safe—they ride the security road and end up with a meaningless life.

Stop dreaming and you start playing it safe. Do that and you won't get involved and you won't run the risk of failure. And, for sure—your life will be dull, drab and dead, totally lacking in energy. The surest and quickest way to permanent fatigue is right there: stop dreaming. But dare to dream and energy will flow like a fresh bubbling mountain stream.

4. FATIGUE COMES FROM PROCRASTINATION
AND INDECISION

There are some who dream a dream but then delay making a decision to do anything about it. Procrastination produces fatigue. Indecision is a fatigue-producing experience. Make a bold decision and see what energy surges from deep within you.

5. Fatigue Rises From Guilt

Is there some secret sin in your life? If so, there will be guilt, and this guilt will block the flow of real power and energy. All you need is one secret, gnawing guilt or sin, and the fear of its exposure can create an emotional block that will greatly reduce your energy output.

The truth is: Only authentic and honest people can be enthusiastic. Guilt saps your enthusiasm. And without enthusiasm there is fatigue.

Why aren't more people genuinely enthusiastic? Because they are not honest. So they have to be careful of what they say. Because they are harboring a secret sin. If you live an open and clean life, then you don't have to be careful of what you say or do. And you will be surprised what enthusiasm is released. And enthusiasm is energy.

6. Fatigue Comes From Negative Vibrations

Negativity that produces fear, anxiety, and anger blocks the creative flow of energy and produces fatigue. Positive thoughts draw power to dream dreams and get us involved in projects. They get us excited—fill us with energy.

Once I was asked to attend a board meeting of a corporation of which I am not a member. In less than five minutes I discovered that a lawyer present was very upset about something. I could tell by the mental climate he was creating that there were such negative vibrations present that I would be fatigued in a matter of minutes. Since I didn't want to waste my energy, I said something to the effect: "When you are able to address yourselves in positive terms with enthusiasm, in a calm and reflective mind, I will be happy to return and re-join the assembly." And with that I made my exit. I could feel the fatigue hanging in the room because of the negative vibrations coming from this cantankerous negative-thinking lawyer.

I came back to the room after a few minutes to find the lawyer storming out. I then suggested to the remaining board members that they get on with dreaming about the project that brought them together. Soon they got excited again. As they started putting forth their ideas, energy returned. And an amazing transformation took place in that room!

7. FATIGUE COMES MORE FROM A BAD ATTITUDE THAN FROM OLD AGE

Energy level is more a matter of attitude than age. I see some people with low energy levels who say, "I guess I must be getting old." I don't believe it. I have seen college students walking slowly, their bodies drooping, and if you tinted their hair white and put some dark spots on their skin to make their skin look old, you would say that they were eighty years old. They walk and they talk old. They feel old.

Obviously, there are differences in energy levels between one person and another. The question is, why? The answer lies more in attitude than age.

Recently I heard that famous and powerful United States

Senator, Hubert Humphrey, deliver a lecture in Miami, Florida. It was a great speech, but what impressed me even more was that this man, in his sixties, had come back from a long battle with cancer, and he still possessed tremendous energy. As I studied him, I was struck with this thought: "Energy is not a matter of age—it's attitude. And an abundance of energy is not a matter of general health, because I see people who have had major surgery and are still battling cancer, and they have loads of energy."

The Keys to Unlimited Energy

There are three keys to unlimited energy. Mark them carefully and you will have a head start toward Supersuccessful living.

1. LIVE RIGHT

Develop a program of physical fitness. When you are too tired to endure physical exercise, the way to get energy is to exercise anyway. After you have run two miles, strength comes. After the third mile, you have more energy. And after the fourth mile, you are ready to go. Obviously you will not find that kind of energy if you are not willing to pay the price of disciplining your own body.

Physical energy is, of course, a matter of keeping your body in good tone and good tune, but it also requires spiritual exercise.

2. LOVE RIGHT

Love is an energy-producing force. When you really love people, you get excited about them and want to help them. You get enthused about projects that help people who are hurting, and this is what produces energy. God will get you so excited about some of the wonderful things to do in this world that you will forget all about yourself and your own problems. You will think about others who have problems and rush to try to help them. That's what gets you totally turned on.

Find something you can give your soul and heart to and get excited about that—and you will have a high energy level.

3. PRAY RIGHT

There can be no doubt that your relationship with God is a vital factor in your own human energy level. Enthusiasm comes from two Greek words, *en theos:* "from God."

Don Sutton, the Los Angeles Dodgers pitcher, has shared with me how every professional athlete looks for an edge. "Because," he said, "to really be a great success, all you have to do is to be just a little better than everybody else. It's that simple. All you need is the edge on the competition." Then he added, "Jesus Christ gives me the winner's edge."

And he does. Because it is God who produces the dynamic flow of energy, St. Paul knew this when he wrote: "I can do all things in him who strengthens me" (Phil. 4:13, RSV).

If you need more energy, it means you need more faith in God, to dream enthusiasm-generating dreams. If you have a close relationship with God you will be dreaming great dreams and attempting great things. Anyone who lives and moves in the will of God is going to be a high-energy person. If you want the energy of God in your life, give your life to God. He will come in and you will be in tune with an infinite cosmic source of unending, unlimited energy that will recycle itself as you do his happy work.

At the end of every day, the last thing I do is to pray, "Father, I have sinned again today." And then I try to think of what, specifically, my sins are, and I confess them. I ask God to forgive me. Then I put my head on the pillow without any twinge of guilt. I have asked for forgiveness, and I know God gives it.

Then I pray for his Spirit to come and fill my life. And because I know he does, I sleep like a baby. If I wake very early in the morning, it is because I'm so enthused and excited about the things I can do for God that I can't wait to get dressed and go to work. Then I begin each new day with this prayer, "Father, it's a brand new day and a brand new life, filled with bright new possibilities." Isn't that exciting?

If you begin and end your day that way you will be charged with positive emotions, because God will be with you to guide you, lead you, and direct you. You are going to get involved, and you are going to get excited, and that produces great energy!

Live right, love right, and pray right. And you will start thinking right. You will be surprised at the energy output that is going to come out of your life.

I don't think anything is more damnable than the idea that you are going to get old, weak, frail, sick, and finally die miserably. It doesn't have to be that way at all. Your life and mine, in the providence of God, are designed to be like a flower. It sprouts, grows, and spreads its branches; it unfolds its leaves, and brings its buds to full flower. And then one morning the petals are gone. And new seed falls to begin new life. That's the way your life was planned—dynamic to the end. And the end will be a new beginning.

Remember this: You are not really alive unless you are enjoying good energy. And God gave all of us the same basic equipment. There isn't much difference between bodies, but there can be a great deal of difference in our relationships with God. There are some people who have a great relationship with him. They are alive with dynamic divine energy that flows through them. You can be that kind of person. You can have this constant recycling of energy when you spend your energy building, constructing, helping, and pursuing great things for God. This in turn makes you more enthusiastic, which then replenishes your energy supply.

Do this and you will develop a life-style that guarantees a constant flow of energy. You will never be fatigued again.

William James said, "You have enormous untapped power that you will probably never tap, because most people never run far enough on their first wind to ever find they have a second."

You can have that beautiful second wind as you keep energy-draining moods out of your life. Master your moods. fill every day with moods and mental outlooks that will unlock new reservoirs of energy.

14 Manage Your Moods or They Will Manage You

But what do you do when the low moods come? And they surely will. The day comes when all that excitement and enthusiasm and energy seem to take a vacation from you. All the highs become lows. How, then, do you keep your enthusiasm up? How do you maintain a high energy level? How do you avoid making irreversible and negative decisions in your low moments? How do you keep your thinking clear and clean, and how do you handle natural difficulties with aplomb?

You have to be prepared for such moments. In this chapter I want to show you how you can manage your moods so that they will not be managing you, for: "He who rules his spirit [is better] than he who takes a city" (Prov. 16:32, RSV).

When I arrived in Minneapolis the plane put down in a blizzard. But the next day the sun was bright and by noon, the snow was beginning to melt. When I arrived at the hall where I was to speak, someone greeted me with, "Dr. Schuller, did you bring this weather with you?"

The truth is: We all bring weather with us wherever we go. We always bring a mental climate, no matter where we travel. Step into a room, meet people, talk with them, and you either bring sunshine or gloom, shadow or sparkling enjoyment. You create a mood wherever you go. The mood you create is the mental climate you bring with you.

So you need to manage those moods, or they will manage you. Here are ten tips that can help you:

1. DETERMINE TO MANAGE YOUR MOODS

Do not look upon the moods that come to you as something out of your control, something you can't handle. You are far more powerful than your moods. You do not need to let a dark spirit rule you. You can rule your own spirit.

There are some days when your moods will not be at their high peak. When that happens, you may need to withdraw from people for awhile. That's what Jesus did. There was a time when the crowd pressed him, and to handle his own mood he withdrew and went into the mountains to pray alone. Do that, and your moods won't manage you.

2. DON'T INTERNALIZE YOUR NEGATIVE MOODS

People with weak egos, who lack security, and consequently overestimate their own significance, never want to admit that they have problems with their moods. So they internalize their feelings. And what happens? Those feelings turn into ulcers or high blood pressure or maybe even a heart attack.

You can internalize your mood in your office, and what happens when you get home? The door slams too hard and you begin to take it out on your children or your wife. And if you keep internalizing those negative feelings at home, you simply won't express love and affection for those around you. To manage your moods, you need to open up, talk it out with a positive-thinking friend, or else you will blow up.

3. GET ACQUAINTED WITH YOUR CYCLES
AND SEASONS

Analyze your moods. If you are touchy, depressed, or anxious, and have vague feelings of worry and fear that you can't pinpoint, try to analyze those feelings. Ask yourself, "Why am I in this mood?" Then ask yourself, "Under whose influence am I when I feel this way?" Perhaps you have been listening to negative thinkers. I hope I don't have to say under *what* influence, and yet I am sure it is true for some of you. Many of you choose to use mood-altering beverages or drugs. The question is: Under *whose* influence do you live? When you are under the influence of God's Holy Spirit, you are on an upbeat. You can be sure of that.

I tell people when they join the Garden Grove Church that there are seasons in life. There is the springtime when faith is born. There is the summer of the maturing of faith. There is the fall, the harvest and the reaping season. And then, inevitably, there is the winter season, the dark time, when you can walk over frozen ground and are sure nothing will grow again.

There are seasons for the soul also. I do not know of a single Christian who can say that his faith has always enjoyed springtime. Everyone has a wintertime of the soul.

Dr. Norman Vincent Peale tells in one of his books how he reached a point where it seemed like his faith was not real to him. Peter Marshall said there was a time when his prayers never seemed to get above the ceiling. The prophets complained of the same thing. We all do.

You need to get acquainted with these low times and simply say, "The tide is out. I will make no decisions now. I will make no commitments. For winter is here and the tide is out. I shall play it cool. I shall wait." And soon the mood of strength will return. Do not be afraid of the low times.

Once, after I had been riding at an emotional peak, I went into a low emotional state, and my wife said, "Well, Bob, this is just a refilling time. You have exhausted your positive emotions and you need a season to replenish and refill." Of course! We all have times when we need to stop, to turn the motor off and refill the inspirational tanks.

Such low times that come are generally very natural and providential. They are God's way of calming you down, making you refill, rethink, realign, get a new perspective, take another check on your values and your goals. Let it happen and the tide will soon come in again.

4. ACCEPT RESPONSIBILITY FOR YOUR MOODS

Whether we recognize it or not, most of our moods are the result of our own activity. St. Paul wrote: "Do not be deceived, for whatever a man sows, that he will also reap" (Gal. 6:7, RSV).

Once there was a little boy who had become angry with his mother after she rebuked him. He ran off into the woods and stood on a hill and yelled into the forest, "I hate you! I hate you!" Then he heard a voice coming back to him out of those woods, "I hate you! I hate you!" The voice scared him and he ran to his mother, crying, "Mother, there is a mean man in the woods. He's yelling that he hates me." His mother took him back to the hill and said, "Shout as loud as you can into the woods, 'I love you, I love you!'" And the voice came back, "I love you, I love you!" So it is with life. Life treats you the way you treat life. Life is an echo.

5. CULTIVATE THE HAPPINESS HABIT

The children in my family are generally even tempered. In part that may be due to the fact that when they were small their mother and I had them memorize the words of Ella Wheeler Wilcox:

> I'm going to be happy today,
> though the skies are cloudy and grey.
> No matter what comes my way,
> I'm going to be happy and gay.

That's the same principle St. Paul taught when he wrote: "Rejoice in the Lord always; again, I will say, Rejoice" (Phil. 4:4, RSV).

Cultivate the happiness habit by helping people who are hurting. There's no better way. My friend, Ben Tee, ran a bootery in Garden Grove. He had the rare skill to custom-build shoes. When he died not long ago, many people told what he had done for them. One story is about a poor family who came to live here shortly before Christmas. The near-penniless father came to Ben Tee's store one day with his crippled son, and asked if Ben could make a special pair of shoes for the boy: "Like the other boys wore." Ben said he could, but this was the busiest time of the year. Finally, he promised to have them ready by Christmas.

But on December 24, when the father came for the new shoes, Ben hadn't even started work on them. When the father returned at 6:00 P.M., Ben still hadn't begun. He had so much work to do, he simply couldn't get to this special job. But then Ben began and he worked through the night, and at three in the morning, Christmas day, Ben phoned the father to come to the store right away. The shoes were finished. Now Ben normally charged $50 or more for a specially made pair of shoes, but to this poor father he said, "Oh, for work like that I ought to get about ten dollars." And he added cheerfully, "Merry Christmas!"

The secret of joyful living is: Jesus first, Others second, Yourself last. I have always found that whenever I had a low time, all I had to do was to go out and make a call on some old or sick person. This works wonders every time.

6. Turn your thinking dial

When my children were young, I used to dial the radio to one program where there was nothing but noise, and then to another where the tones were calm. I would let the radio play the loud ranting of a demagogue, and then switch to beautiful music. Then I would say, "Turn the dial in your own mind. You have a dial that you can set to pick up a new signal. Make up your mind that you are going to be happy today. And if you get some signals that suggest you are not going to be happy, turn the dial." When you have made up your mind to do that, you are well on your way to having beautiful moods.

"As a man thinketh in his heart, so is he," the Bible teaches.

Santayana, the Spanish philosopher, is one of my favorite poets. I think that of all of his lines in prose and poetry, I enjoy his words on faith the most:

> O World, thou choosest not the better part!
> It is not wisdom to be only wise,
> And on the inward vision close the eyes,
> But it is wisdom to believe the heart.
> Columbus found a world, and had no chart,
> Save one that faith deciphered in the skies;
> To trust the soul's invincible surmise
> Was all his science and his only art.
> Our knowledge is a torch of smoky pine
> That lights the pathway but one step ahead
> Across a void of mystery and dread.
> Bid, then, the tender light of faith to shine
> By which alone the mortal heart is led
> Unto the thinking of the thought divine.*

The thinking of a divine thought. Turn your thought dial. Think divine thoughts, for such thoughts will determine your moods and your emotions.

*George Santayana, *Poems* (New York: Scribner's, 1922), p. 5.

When the American forces moved into Italy and liberated a little Italian village, they found that old philosopher, Santayana. The war was going on all around him, but here he was in a back room writing a book. "Sir, how can you be creative enough to write a book when the war is going on all around you?" an American general asked. Santayana answered: "I'm an old man. Through all my life I have been a philosopher. And I have trained my mind to think on eternal matters."

Train your mind that way. Turn your thinking dial to eternal matters and you will conquer those dark moods.

7. USE YOUR BODY TO CHANGE YOUR MIND

It has been established by students of the human personality that even as the mind affects the body, so the body affects the mind. If you feel low, and if you allow your body to get drooped in a chair, you will feel more depressed. What should you do? Stand up straight, stretch your body, take a deep breath, throw your shoulders back, lift your chin up, open your eyes wide, flex your muscles and say, "With the grace of God, I am strong!"

Then put your feet two feet apart, feel your full height, and before you know it your body will begin changing your mood. God created you this way. And it's part of the way in which you fulfill the biblical injunction: "He who rules his spirit is better than he who takes the city."

8. REPROGRAM YOUR MEMORY BANK

Do you know your moods are determined primarily by a recording of past experiences or expectations of future experiences? On a recent trip to an eastern city, I arrived at my hotel about 12:30 in the morning. The young woman who checked me in said offhandedly, as she was getting ready to leave for the evening, "Well, I will take my three aspirins and go."

I asked her, "Why should a lovely lady like you be taking three aspirins at 12:30 in the morning?" Then she began to tell me her story, which was really a collection of emotional and spiritual difficulties out of her past.

She was once with the Ice Capades, "A good skater," she said. But then she married and later divorced. "That's when my problems began," she said, "eight years ago when he divorced me. But that's all past, over and done with."

I said, "I don't think it is over and done with. The fact that you still have the pain, that you still need those aspirins eight years later proves it isn't done with. It is still very much alive."

I then took out a piece of paper and placed a dot on it. "A human life starts with a dot. When you are born the dot is there, and it's the beginning of a brand new tape recording. The tape begins. It records the trauma of your birth, the emotional tactile results of the sensation of a body touching against your body. And then it records the voice of your mother. It records every experience through your life. It never stops. If, by the grace of God, there are happy recordings the first week, the first month, the first year of your life, you have a great thing going. If the emotional experience recorded in the second and third year are basically pleasant strokes, it's still a good recording.

"But here on your tape," I continued, "there is a nasty bit of static and aggravated assault recorded eight years ago. Of course, your tape recorder was still going through that divorce.

Every once in awhile the bitter memories of anguish hurt and ugliness struggles to break through. You repress those negative memories, but they emerge anyway in the form of ugly moods.

"I think what you need to do," I concluded, "is to really accept Jesus Christ into your life as your personal Lord and Savior, in a very real way, and let him heal your memories." So I tried to lead her to Christ.

The next day, at the college where I had given a lecture, a girl came up to me with a copy of one of my books and said, "Will you autograph this for a friend of mine? She's the girl you talked with at the desk last night in the hotel. She called me today and said she met you, and asked me to tell you that things are already changing beautifully."

If your memories are tainted with guilt, hurts, resentments, jealousies, or rejections, don't ignore them. They will bubble up in the form of bad moods. The only way to heal your past is to ask Jesus Christ to come in and cleanse your soiled memories.

9. CLEANSE THE ROOTS OF YOUR SPIRIT

There's a palm tree in front of my house that for a time was yellow at the core. Even though it still had some green fronds, it looked as though it was soon going to die. My florist suggested that it needed (what he called) "deep treatment." He recommended that I inject fertilizer through a long pipe, which could penetrate the ground all the way to the roots. Then he told me to put a hose all the way down to the root level, and then very slowly let the water ooze out. I was to do this day after day. I did, and the tree is prospering today.

I had thought sprinkling the lawn was good enough, but this tree had a special problem that required deep treatment.

Some of you come to church week after week and get the surface sprinkler treatment. For some of you that's enough to keep your spirit as green as watered grass. But many people have a deep problem and need the "deep treatment," the kind of treatment that happens only when you ask the Holy Spirit to come in and fill your life with God himself.

10. GET ON THE RIGHT TRACK

Eliminate negative moods and stimulate positive moods. A negative mood is characterized by a lack of enthusiasm: an apathy, fear, apprehension, anxiety, or a vague neurotic depression—that controls your feelings. When the Spirit of God himself controls you, then you will be dominated by the positive emotions of hope, faith, love, joy—and all these are upbeats! If you are in a low time, the thing to do is to make sure your mind and soul are in harmony with God.

One of the most awesome experiences of my life took place during a train trip from Luvov, Russia, to Vienna, Austria. When my companions and I approached the border between Czechoslovakia and Russia, the train stopped and everybody had to get off. While we were waiting, huge jacks lifted up all the cars of the half-mile-long train. As I watched in amazement, a little pushcart shoved the wheels underneath together like a stack of dominoes. Then from the other end, came another set of wheels, fitting a second set of tracks that were inside the first set. The narrower tracks were designed for Czechoslovakia, of course, so that the Russian trains couldn't come running right through into the country.

Some of you are on a negative-thinking line, and that's why you are moody. Jesus said, "The gate is wide and the way is easy that leads to destruction, and those who enter by it are many. For the gate is narrow and the way is hard that leads to life, and those who find it are few" (Matt. 7:13–14, RSV).

God's railroad track has a positive gauge. Loads of people live a life-style that is like a railroad track that just isn't in God's line-up at all. You are never going to have the touch of God's peace in your soul until you harmonize with God's life-style. Get on God's track. This will help you sterilize and paralyze your negative moods. When you live God's way you live beautifully. And when you don't live God's way, happy moods will be crowded out.

You can't think of a bad thought and a pure thought at the same time. And many of the moods you have are the result of negative thoughts. Many of them are attributable to one little word—*sin*! Now, if you have that problem in your soul, then vitalize your life. Take Christ into your life. That's why Jesus is called Savior. He wants to come inside of you. He died on a cross for you. He wants to save you from sin. He wants to give you a new life. He can turn you into a new person, a new creation.

Are you down? Do you have problems with low moods?

Arthur Rubinstein was once so depressed that he came close to ending his life. But the belt he planned to use to hang himself broke. He fell to his knees, and when he came up he was suddenly surrounded by an awareness of the beauty of life all around him. "I have loved living ever since," he confessed to Barbara Walters in a TV interview. That was a miracle that turned his mood around, a miracle of God's grace.

William Cowper, whose hymns have been sung by Christtians all over the world, has been an inspiration to many. I remember when we went to the little church in Newkirk, Iowa, near my parents' farm home, after a tornado had destroyed almost everything they owned. We went there for a prayer service, because a lot of us were down in our moods. And we sang,

> God moves in mysterious ways,
> His wonders to perform,
> He plants His footsteps on the sea,
> and rides upon the storm.

Those words were written by William Cowper.

William Cowper, himself, was really down one time in his life. And he decided to end it all and carefully planned his suicide. He went to a river, only to find people were standing at the bridge. Then he went into an attic, and tried to hang himself with a rope. But the rope broke. Then he dropped his body on a sword, but the point broke off when it hit a rib. At this point, his testimony, (reading from his diary), says, "I was suddenly overwhelmed by God's presence and love." And he fell on his knees and said, "Oh, Lord, be merciful to me, a sinner. Jesus Christ, save my immortal soul." And new life came to him. He became a new person. He was literally born again.

Now that's God's plan for you. But remember, *it takes two to make a miracle.* You simply say, "It's time for me to make some very deep changes in my life." Then pray, "Oh God, I thank you that I am alive today. I thank you that miracles turn moods around. I feel your presence with me now. Take my life and make it new, consecrated, Lord, to you. Amen."

15 Superpower When Things Don't Work Out

What do you do when life seems to tumble in? You have dared to dream big dreams. You have made great commitments and you are determined never to give up. Then it happens! Your world starts coming apart. What do you do now?

Now you need what I call "Superpower" to keep you going strong. There is such a thing. I have experienced it, and I believe you can have it, too.

Superpower comes to you as you keep thinking positively. Do you believe that? Some people don't. They say:

"You can't keep a positive mental attitude always."
"To be cheerful through life's tragic moments is unreal."
"The perpetual Possibility Thinker is a phony."

These are the claims of a cynic. Are they true or false? I claim they are false, and in this chapter I want to share with you ten principles Possibility Thinkers have discovered that enable them to be cheerful, with sincerity and integrity, through the toughest of times.

1. THERE IS NO GROWTH WITHOUT SEPARATION

"Consider the lilies of the field, how they grow," Jesus said. Well, how do lilies grow? Painfully! Cells begin to swell until they are bloated. Then they burst and separate.

Cells must split in order for growth to occur. The eagle throws her little ones out of her nest so that the young will learn to fly. A child has to leave the crib and eventually the home, and finally the security of the university halls, as he goes out into the world. There is no growth without pain, struggle, separation.

We only grow through struggle and difficulty. The mind grows as it struggles with concepts through reading, researching, and wrestling until finally one day the light breaks through and everything is clear. I remember when my daughter was taking organic chemistry, she thought she would never understand it. But she kept struggling and working, until one day she came home and threw her book up and the papers floated all around. "I see it all! Everything is as clear as day!" she said.

How does one grow into an emotionally whole person? How does the heart grow? By experiencing laughter and tears. By tasting hope and disappointment. By tasting success and failure. This is the growth process that turns us into mature people. Show me a great person and I will show you a person who has been hurt.

2. THERE IS NO MEANING IN LIFE WITHOUT A CHALLENGE

Throughout this book we have been emphasizing a great idea. Problems, we have been saying, create projects, and there is no purpose to life unless there are problems begging solutions. Take the challenge out of life and you have death.

Jackie Gleason once said on a talk show, "All my life it had been tough until I started succeeding. Then one day I found I had everything I wanted. When you have all you have ever wanted and you want nothing more, you end up asking yourself what is the meaning of it all."

St. Paul expressed this challenge: "I press on toward the goal for the prize of the upward call of God in Jesus Christ" (Phil. 3:14, RSV).

3. THERE IS NO CONVERSION WITHOUT CRISES

That's true for plant life when it is converted into animal life. And it is also true for the human soul, which is converted into becoming a believer in God. Conversion, which means being turned around, doesn't happen without crises.

A cynic says: "Oh, yes, he had a conversion to religion, but you see, he lost a son in a tragedy. It's an emotional thing for him."

So what? That doesn't invalidate the experience! There is no conversion without crisis. Possibility Thinkers know this, and that's why when they face a crisis they anticipate that something is going to be converted out of it. And it is going to be great. Just wait and see!

4. There is no way of helping people without hurting them

The doctor cuts in surgery. The dentist drills. The teacher must criticize creatively. The father says, "No!" You cannot help people without hurting them. And you cannot get help without experiencing hurt. *There is no gain without pain.* Consider the spoiled brat as proof of this principle.

5. There is no adventure without risk

We know that if you take the risk out of life and arrive at total security, you will taste total boredom. That is why God doesn't tell us how secure and safe we really are. If God would let you know how truly safe and secure you really are—if he would let you see the future so that you could know that beyond every tragedy there awaits a great blessing, what would happen to you? I will tell you. If God were to remove the creative tension of future uncertainty, you would become so lethargic that you would be emotionally dead. There is no adventure without risk.

6. There are no great movements without great issues

The problems we face in this world are our opportunities to create a new project or to launch a great new movement. But there are no great movements without equally great issues. There are institutions that started out like a ball of fire because they had a great cause, which they tackled in a redemptive way. But when the cause began to pass away, the movement lost its power. Without a great issue, movements, projects, and causes wilt and die.

7. THERE CAN BE NO LIFE WITHOUT CLOUDS

What produces life? The sun? Yes and no. Consider the rain, too. Take away the rain and you have a desert with searing heat. Take away the rain and sunshine becomes a curse. There is no life without clouds. There is no dawning unless there is first a sunset, and then the black of night. Remember: the darker the night, the brighter the sunset.

8. ONE PERSON'S NEED IS ANOTHER
PERSON'S OPPORTUNITY

Once when I was in the hospital with broken ribs and an injured kidney after a horrible fall, I began to wonder what good there could possibly be in this, and what good could come out of it. Several things came to my mind, but I never would have thought of one of the more obvious goods if I had not talked with one of the janitors one night. I was in distress and couldn't sleep. So we talked.

The janitor was a Mexican-American. And he told me about his wife and children, and how happy he was to have such a good job so that he could support them. What a revelation! Because I was in the hospital, this man was earning a living for his family!

It's true! If there were no sick people in need of medical attention, there would be no opportunities for doctors and nurses and janitors, such as this man, to earn a living. If there were no ignorant people, there would be no opportunities for educators. One person's need becomes someone else's opportunity. That insight gave fresh meaning to my confinement and did wonders for my positive attitude.

9. THERE IS NO CREATIVITY WITHOUT CONFLICT

Creativity doesn't just happen. The best actor, the best novelist, the best poet, the best sculptor, the best musician: how do any of them arrive at their success? The path of excellence is a road strewn with the litter of failures, the result of struggle, trial and error, and many dark nights.

In preparing my sermons, I read and struggle continuously. Often I throw away a lot of the material I have prepared. I do more reading, which sometimes seems like a futile search for just the right idea, the right illustration, the right phrase or word. I go through dry periods when nothing creative seems to happen. Then suddenly, a light dawns. Out of the hours of inner struggle an idea forms. And then I say, "Oh, thank you, God, that is a great idea! That will help people!" Creativity often occurs in the deep peace that follows a time of conflict.

10. THERE IS NO RESURRECTION WITHOUT DEATH

Here is a truth of ultimate importance. You are constantly in the process of death and resurrection. Body cells are dying and new cells are being born. So death is a mark of growth. A plant dies! Or does it really die? No, death is only a phase of new life being born in another plant, in fossil energy, in an animal or a fowl.

The truth is, death is not real. It is only a phase of a new life being born. At a funeral recently, I said to the wife and children of the man who had died, "There is nothing but life. *We* are in the land of the dying. *He* is in the land of the living."

These principles are universal, and they give us cause to be optimistic. They explain why things often have to get worse before they can get better. They explain, for instance, why a marriage has to almost die before it can be renewed, for only then will a husband and wife go to a counselor for help. They explain why a wife packs her bag after years of marriage and moves out, before the husband will admit he has a drinking problem and go in tears to AA.

Because we know these principles, we can say with scientific and spiritual integrity that there is a light behind every shadow. Show me a great man and I will show you a man who has been through the shadows. That is why we say there is a purpose behind every problem. God has a design for every difficulty. If you understand these principles you will come to see that the Possibility Thinker is profound and not a Pollyanna in harnessing these principles to produce a positive mental attitude always.

Take a Fling at Real Living

If there is a shadow moving into your life, keep on keeping on. Fling away your tears. Don't be afraid of the shadows.

Did you know that the barnacle, that little creature with

the tough shell in the ocean, which clings to piers, started out with the capability of being free? But it chose security and decided to seize the first thing it could grab hold of, and then it built a hard shell so that it could spend its life kicking food into its mouth with its rear feet. You can be that way, or you can be like the missionaries of the church, who through the centuries have taken a fling at living, seeking adventure, welcoming problems, and saying, "I'll welcome the wind." How can a kite fly without wind?

Take a fling at real living. Don't seek selfish safety and security. I can tell you from my visit with missionaries on a recent trip around the world that they are among the happiest people in the world. And I can think of no professional group that deliberately chooses and faces more problems and difficulties than they do. They decided to take a fling for God and live.

I remember seeing a play several years ago in which a man died and woke up in the afterlife. It was beautiful beyond his expectations. Everything that he wanted was given to him, even before he could ask for it. Every desire was filled even before he knew he had the want. There was no work to do. Finally, in the intolerable boredom of it all, he said to his attendant, "I want something now that I am going to have to work for and wait for." The attendant said, "But that's impossible here." The man said, in anger, "All right, then, I'll go to hell." And the attendant said, "Sir, where do you think you are?"

A member of the Garden Grove Church, who grew up in a wealthy home, said to me one day, "My problem is, I have never known what it is to want anything. My parents traveled.

They had money and they always knew what I wanted before I knew it existed. I wish I could know what it is like to
want something."

Sing When the Shadows Fall

Yes, that's the way to face the black shadows that cross your
life. Sing when a shadow falls across your path. Welcome the
wind. When trouble strikes, you can be sure some good will
come of it. This is your great opportunity to use Possibility
Thinking.

Are you having a conflict with somebody right now? Consider the possibilities. Conflict is an opportunity for you to
say, "I'm sorry." Have you been hurt? That's an opportunity
for you to say, "I love you anyway." Are you a victim of injustice? It is your chance to show how beautiful you can be.
Do you have problems and troubles? This is your chance to
show the world how calm and joyful a Christian can be even
when there is no apparent cause to be happy.

If you have a problem coming to you, I say, without hesitation, get ready to sing. God is getting ready to turn you into
a more beautiful person. The shadow may be an answer to
your prayers. Perhaps God is teaching you how to be hurt
so that you will be more gentle. Perhaps God is letting you
feel the shadows now so that with genuine sympathy and not
phony piety you can really care about other people who are
hurting. Your shadow may be God's way of making you into
the truly beautiful person you always wanted to be. So start
singing!

Let God Release Your Hidden Splendor

It was in Bangkok that I saw a famous Buddha. Until 1955, this ten-foot-high, eight-ton Buddha stood in the courtyard outside a chapel for many years. No one knew where it came from. Legend said that hundreds of years before it had been floated down a river from the North. Now, in 1955, a priest decided to renovate his chapel, and when it was all finished he determined to put the old Buddha in the temple. "After all," he thought, "it's a pity to leave it out there under a tin roof with the rain dripping around the edge of it and the water sloshing around its base."

So a crane was brought in to move this giant concrete Buddha, but when this monstrous sculpture was lifted two feet off the ground, a terrible thing happened. The rope broke and the Buddha crashed down, causing an enormous ugly crack to appear from the shoulder all the way across the chest to the trunk of the body. Then it started to rain. Soon darkness fell. Discouraged, the people went home and the priest decided to patch up the crack later.

The next morning when the priest examined the crack in the concrete, he noticed what he thought was a glimmer of light in the shadow of the crack. He looked more closely, and then discovered that the light he saw was a flash of gold. He began to chip at the concrete with his bare hand until he cracked off a larger chunk. Then he saw a breastplate of gold. He cracked another layer, and exposed more gold. Soon he had clawed the entire concrete veneer off, and there was exposed the world's largest chunk of solid gold. A five-and-a-half-ton solid gold Buddha!

Now we know the story. It was created in 1295 by order of the King of Siam. When the army from Burma was threatening to move in, the people in the little village in the north country, fearful that the golden Buddha would be stolen, covered it with cement in order to hide it. They were all killed, wiped out by the invaders, and nobody knew the secret—that inside this old concrete shell was this golden Buddha. It took a fall to bring out the hidden splendor.

Cling to God's Promise

Do you have a problem? Get set for a blessing. Fling away the fear. Start singing. God is getting ready to bring the hidden splendor out of you. Now cling to the promises of God. "I will never leave you nor forsake you. . . . " "All things work together for good to those that love God and keep his commandments." . . . "Be confident in this one thing, that God has begun a good work in you and will complete it." . . . "He who lives and believes shall never die." Cling to the promises of God.

In an earlier chapter of this book, we mentioned Russell Conwell's famous story of the Golconda diamond mine. Real treasure, the story said, lies right beneath our feet. But perhaps many of you have forgotten the story behind that story.

It happened during the Civil War. Conwell, from Berkshire, Massachusetts, an atheist and a nonbeliever, was the leader of a regiment that was called The Berkshire Boys. Colonel Conwell had led these young volunteers in one victory after another, until one night they found themselves at the edge of a stream where they were caught off guard by the Confederates. After fleeing across a bridge in order to regroup, Conwell discovered he had left his sword on the other side. One of the boys in his company, a teenager named Johnny Ring, volunteered to get it for him.

Johnny Ring found the sword, and started racing back. When he returned to the bridge, he saw that flames were licking the edges of the wooden boards, but he ran through the flames without hesitation. The Confederates, impressed with the boy's courage and heroism, held their fire.

When Johnny Ring reached the other side, he dropped the sword at his commander's feet. He was badly burned, however, and two hours later he died. Just before he breathed his last, Colonel Conwell said, "Johnny, I'm sorry, I'm sorry."

Johnny Ring said, "Don't be sorry. I'm not afraid to die, I know Jesus Christ. He is my Savior. I'm going to be with him. It's all right, Colonel." With his last breath the dying boy looked at him and said, "Are you afraid to die, sir? Do you know Christ, sir?"

Johnny Ring died and beside his body that night the commander knelt down, and in a great moment alone, accepted Jesus Christ as his Savior. Humbly, he said, "Dear God, I give my life to you. I feel your presence. I felt you come into my tent tonight. I know you are real." Then he made a vow, saying, "God, I'm going to be the person Johnny Ring wanted to be, and I am going to work sixteen hours a day, eight hours for me and eight hours for Johnny Ring to live out his life through me."

In fulfillment of his vow in behalf of Johnny Ring, Colonel Conwell later became a minister. In time, he developed the

famous lecture, Acres of Diamonds, which he delivered over
6,000 times. It earned him more than six million dollars, and
with that money he built Temple University in Philadelphia.
He put over 2,000 students through college, seminary, and
medical school. And when he died he left only the house that
he lived in. He said, "It was Johnny Ring doing it through me."

Part of the message of that great address Russell Conwell
was to give spelled out how real diamonds are beneath our
feet. But there was a further message. "If you are looking for
meaning to life, it's in the trouble that God is sending you
now," Conwell said. And "there are acres of diamonds in that
problem you have before you right now."

There's a light behind every shadow. If there is a shadow, there
must be a light somewhere. So, when a shadow moves across
your sky:

- Fling out the fear. Welcome the new adventure.
- Sing the praises of God! He is planning something beautiful.
- Cling to the Promises of God! He is faithful.
- Wing your way! Rise above the storm like the kite wel-
  comes the wind.

16 Release God's Power Within You

You have met some Supersuccessful People in these pages, and you have learned how you can be a Supersuccess also.

The key is inside you this very moment. Jesus said, "The Kingdom of God is within you" (Luke 17:21). *Within you!* You will be a beautiful person. Yes, you! Even if you have had a record of sins, frailties, shortcomings, faults, dents, cracks, bumps, and lumps accumulated through life.

The key is within you. Deep down, under your outer shell, there lies within your heart wings waiting to unfold and stretch. Give yourself wing power. It's there, just waiting to come out.

There is within you a treasure waiting to be discovered. How do you realize that treasure? How can you release God's power?

1. Crack the Crust
Crack the crust that keeps God's power locked deep within you. The accumulation of negative experiences forms an invisible

crust of hidden memories that chokes, stifles, and suffocates the power that lies deeper—waiting to erupt with renewing enthusiasm. All of your rejections, failures, hurts, setbacks, and defeats tend to accumulate like encrustations around your inner spirit. You have to crack that crust off.

There is a small town down on the Pacific coast where I go frequently to read, to pray, and to write. Here the ocean crashes against the huge rocks along the shoreline. I like to walk down to the tidal pools and watch the sea as it washes in.

It was during my first season there that I became fascinated watching the whales move South. Huge California gray whales, averaging forty tons in weight, move slowly along the coast. One day I heard an awful thrashing and I saw what looked to be a grounded whale. He was thrashing against the rocks with a ferociousness that amazed me. A monster of a whale! I have never been so close to such a large beast in my life. I was alarmed, thinking the whale was hung up on the rocks. So I called the county department that handles animals and explained what was happening. When I told them where I was, they said, "Oh, no, that whale isn't grounded. That's a favorite spot where the whales stop to get rid of their barnacles."

Sure enough. From his months at sea barnacles had accumulated, until a crust had built up, and he had to thrash and grind and rub and scrape until they broke off.

Crack the crust on your fears, your hurts, and your rejections, and let God's positive thoughts flow into your mind.

2. GET IN TUNE
Get in tune with God's spirit. Once you have cracked the crust, he can move in if you are in tune with him—if you are close

enough to God to hear his signals. That means prayer, Bible reading, meditation, and sharing in the fellowship with other Christians.

I have a favorite radio station that I listen to in Southern California. When I travel away from home, one of the things I miss most is that I can't hear my favorite music station. Is the station dead? Is it not functioning? Or is my radio no good? No, everything is in working order. It's just that I am too far away to pick up the signal, that's all.

Some of you will never discover God's power until you get close enough to hear his signals communicating to you.

3. GET IN LINE

Get in line with God's will. Obey him. How do you obey God? By listening to positive thoughts and by refusing to listen to negative thoughts. It's that simple. God will speak to you through positive thoughts. The negative voice that tempts you is not his.

On a visit to Kansas, I went to the home of a distinguished person. On the front door of his beautiful home was taped a crude piece of cardboard. The sign said, "When you pass through this door, speak only positive thoughts or keep quiet."

I wonder what would happen to family life, to the divorce rate, to the response of children in the home, if that were the rule in every home in the United States.

There is a more beautiful you waiting to come through. Crack the crust of your negativity. Get in tune. Get in line. Do this and you will discover the experience of a vital and deep religion.

As he came to the end of his life, Carl Jung, who was un-questionably one of the greatest psychiatrists in history, wrote:

During the past thirty years, people from all civilized countries over Europe have consulted me. I have treated many hundreds of patients. Among all my patients over the age of thirty-five, there was not one whose problem in the final analysis was not that of finding a religious outlook on life. It is safe to say, then, that everyone of them fell ill because they lost that which the living religions of every age had given to their followers. And I would say that not one patient in thirty years under my care was ever really healed unless he regained a healthy, religious outlook.

How can you realize God's power within? How do you have that experience of deep vital religion?

By *using positive foundation stones*—powerful promises from God. Listen to them:

- "Even though I walk through the valley of the shadow of death, I will fear no evil" (P.23:4).

- "Surely goodness and mercy shall follow me all the days of my life" (P.23:6).

- "Thou therefore endure hardness as a good soldier of Jesus Christ" (2 Tim.2:3).

- "(Our God) by the power at work in us is able to do far more abundantly than all that we ask or think" (Eph. 3:20).

- "All things work together for good to those that love God" (Rom. 8:28).

- "Who shall separate us from the love of Christ? Shall tribulation, or distress, or persecution, or famine, or nakedness, or peril, or sword? Nay, in all of these things we are more than conquerors through him that loves us" (Rom. 8:35, 37).

- "Be faithful until death, and I will give you a crown of life" (Rev. 2:10).

- "I can do all things through Christ who strengthens me" (Phil. 4:13).

- "If God be for me, who can be against me?" (Rom. 8:31).

To release God's power within you, I urge you not to depend upon my sentences; or those of other religious leaders; or other counselors and advisors. The foundation of your faith must be God's promises. I can't think of any more powerful foundation stones than those I have just given you.

After you've developed positive foundations, then *harness the superpower of positive affirmations.* Here are several that will help you:

- *Affirmation No.* 1: "I affirm that I will never be defeated, because I will never quit."

- *Affirmation No.* 2: "I affirm that God expects me to be tough-minded, and I am."

- *Affirmation No.* 3: "I affirm that God is stronger and bigger than my problem." [Believe me, he is!]

- *Affirmation No.* 4: "I affirm that God has people all lined up waiting to help me at the right time, in the right place, and they will show up; people I don't even know and have never met."

- *Affirmation No. 5*: "I affirm that God will turn my worst times into my best times and my scars into stars."

- *Affirmation No. 6*: "I affirm that I can never fall away from God's love."

- *Affirmation No. 7*: "I affirm that if I'm totally dedicated I'll eventually win."

When David Nelson was in high school, he became afflicted with a disease that deteriorated his body. The prognosis was not good. The disease would gradually get worse. He was told that he would never finish high school, since he was unable to walk any more, and was put in a wheelchair. His classmates, motivated by his courage, decided to help him. They carried him in his wheelchair up the steps into his classrooms. His graduation became a goal of the entire class.

This went on day after day, month after month, until June finally arrived and his class graduated. There was David Nelson in his cap and gown. And when his name was called out for his diploma, two of the football players picked him up, wheelchair and all, and carried him up the steps onto the platform. As he received his diploma the whole class stood and cheered, as if the class were saying, "We did it, David, didn't we!"

David Nelson has released God's power, and that makes him a Supersuccess. If he can make it, so can you.

•   •   •

This letter came in the mail recently:

Dr. Schuller:
A year ago I was a lost soul entangled in drugs. Then I was caught selling them and was sent to prison. In prison I watched you on television, and I accepted Jesus Christ. Now I am out and experience a rich, wonderful life working for Christ. I strongly believe that he has his hand on me now.

I wish I could see you close enough to shake your hand and kiss your cheek. It is so true what you say—"You can be the person you want to be."

Another Supersuccess story! Another person who released God's power within himself. So can you.

Wherever you are, in a hospital, in a home, or in a motel, I invite you now to do what these people have done. Accept Jesus Christ into your life and you will feel the power of God like you have never felt it before. And his presence in your life will safeguard your success.

Remember again our definition of success: "Success is building self-esteem in yourself and others through service."

Stay Away from Empty Promises

But now a word of warning: While we have been defining success in a very special way, there are forces in society that will tempt you, that will play some mean tricks on you under the alluring promise of "success."

Dr. Clovis Chapel once told of a Sunday School class Christmas party. One member of that class was a severely retarded boy, who eagerly waited for his name to be called when the gifts were given out. When the last gift had been given and his name was still not called, the boy broke into tears. At that moment the Santa Claus went behind the tree and pulled out a large box that had been carefully gift wrapped. The boy seized the box, tore off the ribbons and the wrapping paper. He opened the box, and then despair replaced his sudden joy. The box was empty. Everybody broke out laughing. Somebody had decided to play a prank on this poor fellow. He turned it upside down, shook it, hit the bottom, and still nothing came out. Everybody roared. And the boy walked out of the room quietly, head drooping, shoulders bowed and tears pouring down his face.

What a dirty trick? Yes, but some of you have been tricked just as badly. You didn't know any better. An immoral society came to you with a beautiful gift, all wrapped in colorful ribbons. It promised all you thought you wanted, but you were disillusioned. There was really nothing, nothing of importance, in your own special gift box.

I have mentioned Dr. Victor Frankl several times in these pages. Some time ago he wrote in one of his publications about the pleasure kick Americans are on:

I notice in America everybody is on a pleasure kick. I declare to you, that those who make pleasure their main goal in life are doomed to failure. Man is no longer told by his driving instincts what he must do. He is no longer told by traditional values what he must do. Those who no longer know what they must do, who have no purpose in life, will fall victims to conformity, doing what others do and pleasure will not fulfill them.

He might have added that others will fall victim to totalitarianism, doing what others want them to do. Materialism, pleasure – these do not satisfy. They are only gift-wrapped boxes. They trick us and in the end defeat us.

•   •   •

In 1923, a very important meeting was held at the Edgewater Beach Hotel in Chicago. Attending this meeting were nine of the world's most successful financiers. Those present were:

The president of the largest independent steel company
The president of the largest utility company
The president of the largest gas company
The greatest wheat speculator
The president of the New York Stock Exchange
A member of the president's cabinet
The greatest "bear" in Wall Street
The head of the world's greatest monopoly
The president of the Bank of International Settlements

Certainly we must admit that here was gathered a group of the world's most successful men – at least men who had found the secret of making money.

Twenty-five years later, let's see where these men were:

The president of the largest independent steel company died bankrupt and lived on borrowed money for five years before his death.
The president of the greatest utility company died a fugitive from justice and penniless in a foreign land.
The president of the largest gas company is now insane.
The greatest wheat speculator died abroad, insolvent.

The president of the New York Stock Exchange was recently released from Sing Sing.

The member of the president's cabinet was pardoned from prison so he could die at home.

The greatest "bear" in Wall Street died a suicide.

The head of the greatest monopoly died a suicide.

The president of the Bank of International Settlement died a suicide.

Someone observed the above facts and said: *All of these men learned well the art of making money, but not one of them learned how to live.*

The Highest Success

What is the highest success you can have? It is letting God's love and power flow through you. That's not only the secret of success, it is also the secret of happiness.

Some years ago our world lost a great man, Maurice Chevalier. He was a Christian who believed it was his call in life to cheer up people. "Cheering up people," he said, "is a boomerang activity. It just comes bouncing back at you." His advice to all of us is: "All you have to do is to look around; there are lots of targets. Take aim and let go." Giving cheer to others was Maurice Chevalier's way of being a witness to God.

Frank Laubach once likened the human being to a common sprinkler head on the lawn. "It's worth about eighty cents," he said, "but attach the sprinkler head to a hose, let the water flow through, and it makes flowers grow, and the grass green, and parks in which children can play."

"Your life," Laubach continued, "is God's plan for you to be a sprinkler head for Jesus Christ." Jesus said: "Out of you shall flow rivers of living water." This is God's purpose for you, whoever you are, wherever you are. You can be a soul through which Jesus Christ can spread his love and joy. Here is the purpose that satisfies. Nothing else can compare with that. All other purposes, no matter how beautifully packaged, are by comparison like a trick played by a cruel world on an idiot.

You may remember the story of Helen of Troy, the beautiful queen who, according to legend, was captured, carried away, and became a victim of amnesia. Everybody thought she was dead, but Menelaus was determined to find out if she was dead or alive. He searched for years, until one day he found a wanton wench of a woman, a prostitute. In her wickedness she tossed her head in a certain way, a mannerism that could only be that of Helen of Troy. Menelaus went up to her and said, "Helen, Helen! You are Helen of Troy!" Dawning came back to her, and she knew who she was. She was redeemed.

Enlarging on that story, J. Wallace Hamilton once said: "So Jesus Christ is walking the highways of life looking for the riffraff, looking for the sinners like you and me. Hounding us until He catches us, not to point an accusing finger, but to remind us who we are. Children of God, for whom He died, whom God wants to use as his princess in His kingdom."

I invite you to enjoy the Supersuccessful feeling of self-esteem that comes when you let God's powerful love flow freely out of your life touching the lonely and hurting lives around you.

I invite you to become a joyful Christian. What's that?

A Christian is a mind through which Christ thinks.
A Christian is a heart through which God loves.
A Christian is a hand through which Christ helps.
A Christian is an ear through which Christ listens.
A Christian is a voice through which Christ speaks.

Here's to your Supersuccess!